Vance
York

WHO'S ON FIRST?

Verbal and Visual Gems from the Films of Abbott & Costello

Edited by Richard J. Anobile

Introduction by Carol Burnett

Preface by Howard Thompson

Darien House Inc.

DISTRIBUTED BY W.W. NORTON & COMPANY, INC., NEW YORK, NEW YORK

Pictures and dialogues from the following films are
used with the permission of Universal City Studios, Inc.

Buck Privates
Buck Privates Come Home
In the Navy
Keep 'em Flying
It Ain't Hay
In Society
Hit the Ice
Here Come the CoEds
Naughty Nineties

ISBN 0393 08535 X

Library of Congress Catalogue Card Number: 72-88688

Designed by Harry Chester and Alexander Soma

Printed in the Unted States of America.

Table of Contents

Introduction by Carol Burnett 7

Preface by Howard Thompson 11

Notes by Richard J. Anobile 13

Buck Privates 16

Buck Privates Come Home 62

In the Navy 80

Keep 'em Flying 140

Hit the Ice 158

It Ain't Hay 177

In Society 186

Naughty Nineties 219

Here Come the Co-Eds 244

FOR BUD ABBOTT

Introduction by Carol Burnett

certain types of comedy, but, I repeat, I really do love slapstick. I think it's an art. I happen to think that Abbott and Costello were past masters at it . . . the falls and the schticks that they came up with were incredible. With Laurel and Hardy, you look at some of those old things and you see them today and people scream at them. But if they watch Abbott and Costello, they would say, oh, wasn't that corny?

That's one reason I think a book such as "Who's on First?" is such a valuable record on the fabulous funnymen, Abbott and Costello. Frankly, I believe a book like this one is long overdue, and I hope that today's generation will see it, and when they perceive its unique treatment, and what a great contribution these two comedians made to our lives and times, it will, I hope, bring about a resurgence of interest in them.

You can call me prejudiced, because I suppose I am where Abbott and Costello are concerned. I think that they're classic. Possibly they are not up there now with the Marx Brothers, and with W. C. Fields because there hasn't been enough time. Usually, it happens quite a few years later. Right now, they're contemporary in a sense. Fields was before I was born, and so were Laurel and Hardy. Sometimes comedy actors are like the great old painters — they're not appreciated until a number of years have gone by. But I would say that Abbott and Costello will be recognized for their uniqueness sooner than later.

In addition to the artistry involved, there are difficult aspects to performing when one is part of a team. It's like a marriage, and performers will find they are spending more time with each other than they are with their wives — especially when they are on the road doing personal appearances, night-clubs, and that sort of thing. And eventually comedy teams seem to split, maybe for good reasons,

I guess you would have to say I'm a nut about Abbott and Costello.

I think that they were artists, and I confess I don't understand this tendency in some circles to sort of just put them down as slapstick comics of yesterday. Of course, they engaged in slapstick, but then so did Charlie Chaplin, so did W. C. Fields, and the Marx Brothers.

I love slapstick, and I have used it on my own series on CBS.

Somebody asked me once if I had been influenced in my work by Abbott and Costello. I told them that subliminally, I imagine, I've been influenced by a lot of people, because I'm a fan of maybe because the partners are just tired of it. And that's what happened with Abbott and Costello, just as it has to others, including Dean Martin and Jerry Lewis.

Abbott and Costello were a team from 1937 to 1956, although there was a time in 1945 when they wouldn't talk to each other. I recently read an interview Lou Costello gave in 1958 — the year before he died. In it, he talked candidly, very much so, about his situation with Abbott. Here is what Costello said about that period:

"We split the first time — in 1945 — over a really ridiculous thing. I had fired a maid. I had three maids working for me, and when I refused this one a raise, she held meetings in my home, so I fired her. She went to work for Abbott. I explained to Bud why I let her go, and asked him to fire her, but he wouldn't. So we had a fight — just as we were leaving on a personal appearance tour. We wouldn't talk to each other except when we were on stage.

"Then in 1956 we split because Abbott likes to relax and take it easy, while I've got itchy shoes; I don't like to sit around. The second split was friendly, and I saw more of Bud after we split than before."

In that interview, Costello observed, "when you're a team, there's a lot of worrying about each other; now that's gone." I knew he was right, but I was sorry to see that wonderful team break up.

Incidentally, in that interview, Costello told how he almost became a dramatic actor in movies once, something I hadn't known before. He recounted that at one time Charles Chaplin was his houseguest, escaping from the press which was hounding him. Costello told the interviewer, "Charlie told me he planned to remake 'The Kid,' with me playing the role he created. Then I guess the thing was dropped because he got involved in this political situation, and left the country." Costello was a superb comedian, but I'm sure he also would have been a great dramatic actor, particularly in a picture supervised by Chaplin.

I have been asked if I find any of today's comedians who have been influenced by Abbott and Costello. I really don't know. But I do know that Shecky Greene was a big fan of Costello's and impersonates him in his act. He looks a little like him, too, and he loved Costello very much.

But there are very few performers around who remind me of Abbott and Costello. One who does

is Tim Conway, whose potential has not been realized. The man is a comedy genius. I think Tim, had he been in silent films, would have been as big as any of them. He comes up with incredible pieces of business; he's a brilliant schtick artist, an almost lost art. Woody Allen is cerebral, but he also does a lot of funny business in schtick. I really love the physical business that he comes up with. Physical comedy appeals to me; it's universal. You don't have to listen to anything; you don't even have to understand the language. Physical comedy actors are funny people: They walk funny, they talk funny, they are innately funny. They were born that way.

I want to borrow once more from Lou Costello's remarks in that interview in 1958, when he made this observation: "Slapstick's on the way out, and TV had a lot to do with it. Tastes have changed. The majority isn't buying broad comedy now." What that funny little fat man said was true in 1958 because that was the period when the public seemed to have enough of slapstick. And yet, we use it in my television series and we get some of our biggest laughs that way.

My love affair with Abbott and Costello began when I was a kid, and I remember that "Buck Privates" was the first picture of theirs I saw. I was in grammar school and in junior high school when they were tops in their field. But I never missed them because they made me laugh.

I had a particular love for Costello. Maybe I was drawn to him because he was the underdog, as most of the kids in the audience were. We would scream and laugh at him, but there was an innate sweetness he had that drew me to him. I was bright enough to realize, and I think I'm right in saying this, that Abbott was about the best straight man that ever lived. He fed him beautifully. Let me add, at this particular period in my life, I wasn't interested in show business. I just knew they were great.

Maybe it was because of their background in burlesque and vaudeville, but Abbott and Costello had a certain rare relationship with the audience. People loved them whether they saw them on stage, in movies or on television. You don't find that rapport much these days.

Another thing they had — that Costello had — was empathy. I find that I don't empathize with every clown. I can look at them and say they're funny, but I truly loved that little fat man. I felt like I knew him. A lot of clowns are frightening, but he wasn't. There was a loveliness, an inner beauty that he had that never frightened me.

It's funny, but I just finished a movie, "Pete 'n' Tillie", with Walter Matthau, and we made it at Universal studios — the same place where Abbott and Costello starred in their pictures when they were the highest paid performers in Hollywood. One of the big moments in our film comes when Walter plays the "Who's on First?" routine for our son. It's a very important scene in the movie. It's not visual; it's the record. In the scene, I ask Walter what he is doing, inundating this poor little child with that silliness. He says, "Abbott and Costello are not silly. This is ART." And he teaches the kid the "Who's on First?" routine.

You don't see the Abbott and Costello movies on television as often as you do those of Fields, the Marx Brothers and Laurel and Hardy, but they are on, and I always try to watch them. Now, I watch them from a performer's standpoint, but I still am entertained. I have a more objective viewpoint about them, but I still find them totally charming.

Looking back at their movies, I would say the plots were ridiculous. They always had a subplot of the boy and the girl, which is just boring until the film gets back to the good stuff with them. Their genius is still very basic. It's very honest and pure. I don't think it's any hokier than what people are raving about today.

Dean Martin and Jerry Lewis came to Hollywood and the movies, and they clicked very big and eclipsed Abbott and Costello. Jerry was even crazier at the time, and that's what appealed to a lot of kids. It was somebody new, and Dean could be more of a romantic interest than Abbott. You could get the boy/girl plot in there and not have it as a subplot after the two of them. I still laugh at them.

But there is nothing very mysterious or strange about Martin and Lewis replacing Abbott and Costello as the top comedy team in the country. After all, the history of show business is one of stars being succeeded by others, as the public tastes change for various reasons. It comes with the territory, as everybody in our business knows or should know.

Especially in show business, people tend to lose their perspective. Why, when Martin and Lewis called it quits, considering all the tumult and furor which followed, you would have thought that they were committing professional suicide, at the very least. But look what happened. Each one went his own way, and each one has done very well since.

But what really counts is whether a performer is so good that he leaves behind rich memories of those talents which are remembered generations later. Few are that good, but among those I would certainly put Abbott and Costello. I predict that your kids and mine will be laughing at them, and so will their kids. The word "genius" is too loosely used in our business, but I don't have the slightest reluctance to apply it to them.

Some people say once you've seen one of their films, you've actually seen them all, with the same dialogue sometimes. My answer to this one is, look at all of them — Fields, the Marx Brothers, they're all the same thing. If you liked the person, you bought it. If you didn't, you'd only see it once. It's like kids listening to records constantly. They know every single note in the orchestration and they like to hear it because they know what's coming. It's imbedded in their gray matter. I think all kids love that. Most kids love to hear the same fairy tale over and over again, because they know what's coming and they don't want you to deviate one word. The more of that familiar stuff Costello did, the more I loved it.

In fact, too many people overlook the fact that where stars are concerned, it's not true that familiarity breeds contempt. No, indeed. Particularly where comedy stars are involved. Let's face it. Each one has his own bag of tricks, whether it's a funny little man like Lou Costello, or a mugger like Jerry Lewis. I've noticed an interesting thing usually happens when a star decides that he has been doing his particular thing for too long, and wants a change of pace. It's the old story, the comedian wanting to be a dramatic actor, the actor wanting to be a comedian. But sometimes, when they make this switch, the public rejects them. Maybe that star has gotten tired of his tricks, and maybe his friends or agent have persuaded him that, as the saying goes, it's time for a change. But if the public says no, it's not what they wanted or expected, and if any entertainer insists on going against the public will, he had better get out of the business, or go back to his first bag of tricks.

That's another of the keys to the success of Abbott and Costello. You knew when you saw them it would be the same, familiar format — the same combination of the fumbling, loveable little fat man and the straight man. They never tried to be anything else. They didn't change their image, as the Madison Avenue salesmen call it these days, not when they moved from vaudeville to movies, to guest appearances on television variety shows, and later in their own series.

Abbott and Costello were two very funny men, and I would imagine that for them this is the nicest description which could be applied. But it's true, to a degree not yet generally realized, and that's why I am convinced that in the years ahead, when their movies and television shows are re-used and re-issued, they will will be recognized as classic artists in their field.

I will make the prediction that when that time comes, there will be Abbott and Costello Film Festivals held in various countries throughout the world. They will become tomorrow's "in" thing. Don't forget for a moment that because their comedy is broad, is physical, it's a universal language. But beyond this lies the strong self-identification inherent in the Abbott and Costello movies, plus the empathy I've mentioned. It is often said everybody loves a fat man, and if you will add Costello to this saying, I join with Amen.

I think there is a tendency to downgrade slapstick, a kind of snobbery which implies it's inferior comedy. This isn't always true, but it's a situation that does exist. My friend, Lucille Ball, is an expert at this kind of comedy, and her great talents are acknowledged by everybody here. Everybody loves Lucy.

Abbott and Costello had a uniqueness, a quality that doesn't come around too often in show business. The people recognized it, and they loved them. Somebody who saw them years ago in a personal appearance told me that they sparked an excitement, that the thousands who filled the auditorium

loved everything they said, everything they did. They had a real appeal, the lean straight man, and the funny little fat man, the kind of appeal that is enduring.

"Who's on First"? is the name of this book. As far as I'm concerned, when they ask "who's on first?", I'll answer, "why Abbott and Costello, of course." Who else can you think of who came up with as funny, as zany, and as unforgettable a classic routine?

Comedy and tragedy are intermingled, something too few people realize. There was the memorable Charlie Chaplin, certainly a comedy genius. But when you think about his pictures — and who hasn't seen those revivals? — you realize, you suddenly become aware that it was that wistful, almost tragic quality of his which he so expertly blended with comedy for laughs. Heartbreak and howls may seem far apart, but actually they are not.

It was the same with Abbott and Costello. Of course, there was the broad comedy, the slapstick, the funny little guy being put upon by Abbott. But beneath it all was this subtle layer of tragedy, the little Mr. Average Man who is waging his own fight against the world. Again, always using it as the backdrop, with comedy as the goal. A lot of comedians are aware of this, and try to capture that same quality, but only a few succeed.

I realize that I'm showing quite a partiality to comedians, I suppose because comedy is my business. But to me, making the public laugh is a highly important and very personal thing. And I can't think of anybody who was better at it than Abbott and Costello.

Preface
by HOWARD THOMPSON, film critic and reporter, *The New York Times*

"Eve," announced Bette Davis with withering sarcasm, "would ask Abbott to give her Costello."

Bette was saying a mouthful, thanks to Joseph L. Mankiewicz' pearly script. The line got laughs then and still does on the late show. Here, back in 1950, was "All About Eve", the very quintessence of Hollywood sophistication, not only acknowledging the reign of the Kings of Corn but suggesting that an Abbott and Costello split was unthinkable. Indeed it was. The boys still had six years to go before the cameras. After their last picture, "Dance With Me, Henry", best described as a picture in motion, Costello (the fat one) checked out of things for good.

The fact is, rather curiously, that today one of the most famous and profitable comedy teams in the annals of show business has been left hanging high and dry. You'll never find one of their thirty comedies shown on television after sundown, unlike a wide-audience slot for an "All About Eve." A. and C. pix are carefully, if regularly, relegated to early morning, throwaway run-offs, at least here in New York.

No, the boys have been pretty much ignored in the current nostalgia stampede. While we're all mooning over the golden days of Busby Berkeley musicals, the Eddy-MacDonald lark-fests, along with Cagney, Bogart and the Marx Brothers, nobody really seems to give a nostalgic damn about a pair of old-time burlesque comedians who served up plain, unbuttered, piledriver corn in take-it-or-leave-it style. Yet we took it — and how we took it! Apparently when we all needed it.

After a weak Hollywood start, their second film and the first in which they starred, the 1941 "Buck Privates", almost made Abbott and Costello a national institution overnight. Produced for $200,000 (peanuts then, canary seed now), the picture eventually grossed around $10,000,000. And Universal — and the boys — started grinding them out like sausage. Sausage sold.

The timing of "Buck Privates" was exquisite-ly fortuitous. Wartime America was cramming movie theaters as never before (or since).

Men in uniform (including this one) virtually clung to post theaters for escapist diversion, under the specter of shipment overseas. Laughter counted. And here were two barn-broad comics shovelling out hoary old gags about Army recruitment, something that at least everybody could understand. None of your genteel "See Here, Private Hargrove" stuff, not with straight man Abbott sardonically doing his thing while chunky Lou mugged, grimaced, squealed and ran amok.

The corn was green and somehow reassuring to a country that likes to think it can laugh at itself in any crisis, war or peace. Abbott and Costello had churned up a simple trademark of enforced absurdity. The public flocked.

However you appraise them, Abbott and Costello were the screen's No. 1 comedy team of the Forties and into the Fifties, when their popularity began to dim. For much of this time they were, the *only* successful pair of movie comics. The Brothers Marx hit their peak in the Thirties and tapered off, apparently short of ideas, in the Forties as A. and C. came in. Crosby and Hope, for all their adroit, gold-mine badinage, could hardly be called clowns. And Martin and Lewis got into the comedy act later in 1949 with "My Friend Irma."

The titles of the Abbott and Costello movies tell the whole story. "In the Navy", "Keep 'Em Flying", "Hold That Ghost" — all made out in 1941, after "Buck Privates" — spoke for themselves. So did such later titles as "Lost In a Harem", "The Naughty Nineties", and "Africa Screams". Likewise two of their musicals, "Rio Rita," a hearty trouncing of the stage antique, and "Mexican Hayride", which scuttled Cole Porter's sophisticated score from Broadway and let Lou battle the bull, a live one, which is more than Bobby Clark did on Broadway.

Let's credit Abbott and Costello for more than slapstick corn. They could be surprising. For instance, "Buck Privates Come Home", a sequel that came six years afterward, had genuine warmth and rounded appeal, as the boys tried to smuggle a cute little French orphan into the country aboard a troopship. The boys toned down their knockabout antics tactfully for "Jack and the Beanstalk" (1952); the fairy tale emerged unscathed.

The third novelty, at least looking back, was their first movie, "One Night in the Tropics" (1940). The boys weren't screen stars yet. The A. and C. act was the same, in a festive production with some lovely Jerome Kern tunes, but siphoned into an airy story centering on two pairs of sweethearts.

Like many a Hollywood success, including the great Garbo, the two comedians were treading shallow water as their joint career neared its end. They had already "met" Frankenstein. Now it was "Abbott and Costello Meet the Killer Boris Karloff" (who?), then a head-on collision with the Invisible Man. By 1956, with their sign-off, "Dance With Me Henry", the well seemed to have run dry.

They had come a long way, at least geographically, from burlesque. In both 1942 and 1943 they were voted the box-office champs over such rivals as Clark Gable, Bette Davis and Betty Grable. They were reportedly millionaires, stemming from a file of over 2,000 stock comedy situations older than Methuselah. In 1944 alone they personally earned $789,628 team-wise, topped in the entire country only by Louis B. Mayer, chief rajah of Metro-Goldwyn-Mayer.

The two men had first met, subsequently teaming, in a burlesque showcase in Brooklyn in the early Thirties. Born in Paterson, New Jersey, on March 6, 1906, Costello (Louis Francis Cristillo) headed for Hollywood when he was nineteen and after lean times as a young studio laborer and stuntman headed back east. Burlesque first beckoned in St. Joseph, Missouri, with a $16-a-week job as a "Dutch" comic.

Abbott, ten years older, was born in Asbury Park, New Jersey, of a show-biz family. He grew up in the business and became a well-known straight man for Minsky comics before linking with Costello. But burlesque strippers were edging out clowns. The team landed in Hollywood via two and a half years on Kate Smith's radio show and a Broadway revue, "The Streets of Paris" (also Carmen Miranda's springboard to the West).

Reportedly, the two men were friends off-screen as well as on and never held a joint contract in writing. At one point, they almost split but the rift, a widely-publicized one, was healed. Both were family men living in lavish comfort. In later years, they briefly tried a radio series, then a television series (one critic said "the medium was much newer than their material") and independent production of their trickling features. Costello succumbed to a heart attack in 1959 and was survived by his wife and three daughters. The team had officially announced a friendly dissolvement of their partnership two years before.

The party is over, so is the act and all those Abbott and Costello movies linger on, at least on television. Mornings. Or early afternoons. None of your prime time for these two relics.

In the current stampede over the bygone Golden Days of Hollywood and full-fledged movie stars of yore, let's not ignore a public-supported national institution. Abbott and Costello had no illusions about art. They made us laugh. Let's never dismiss them, not as long as our children love them.

Notes on
WHO'S ON FIRST?

by Richard J. Anobile

Curiously enough, my fondest memories of film comedy are those of Abbott & Costello. I say 'curiously enough' because of all the screen comedians, Abbott & Costello seem to be the most easily dismissed. But when I was growing up in the '40's and '50's they were the reigning comedians. W. C. Fields and the Marx Bros. were already out of the limelight and my appreciation of their humor was to come years later only when retrospectives of their works began springing up around the U.S. Bud Abbott & Lou Costello filled the void and from 1941 until the early '50's, they were *the* comedy team. Their humor is now dated and far from the sophistication demanded by today's film audience. However, bearing in mind their time and place allows us to appreciate them today.

Abbott & Costello's slapstick comedy was such that their appeal was distinct. They were throwbacks to vaudeville and burlesque, which, in fact, was where they had their roots. By the time the team made it to Hollywood, Hitler was waging war and America, still trying to break loose from the grip of depression, was forced to send an army to fight the enemies. Americans, already burdened with hardship, now found their problems compounded and sought avenues of escape. Abbott & Costello provided that escape. With the release of BUCK PRIVATES in 1941, Bud and

Lou became the darlings of America. They reminded people of happier days and pumped out two and three films a year, all hungrily consumed by film-going Americans.

Looking back to the period, one realizes that they could only have survived when they did. It was perfect timing. In viewing their films, one can sense the mood and spirit of America. As we began to slip into the '50's, America's personality began to change. The country was congratulating itself for a war well won. The Senate was hunting "subversives". The Atom Bomb had arrived and America lost its innocence. Hollywood was thrown into a depression all its own and Abbott & Costello no longer filled a need. The team lingered on, but with the arrival of Martin & Lewis it was evident that the fickle film audience was switching allegiance.

Yet, they are still around today. As TV began to change the face of the entertainment business it had relied on the tried and true talents of movie personalities. For years in the early '50's Abbott & Costello had their own weekly half-hour series and those shows, along with their films, are still playing the tube today. The audience is younger, but none the less it is substantial and appreciative and possibly a bit more objective than other audiences.

Bud Abbott & Lou Costello filled a need.

They were a phenomenon of their time and because of this they deserve to be remembered today .

* * *

This book is totally comprised of frame blow-ups taken directly from the original films. In compiling this volume I was again reminded of the current apathy surrounding Abbott & Costello when I began looking into the materials I required. Not one Abbott & Costello feature has been transferred from the dangerous nitrate stock (highly inflammable) to a safety stock for preservation. When my film editor in New York City received the fine grains he pointed out to me that the image had shrunk. In time, little by little, the image will pull back from the celluoid and flake off until nothing is left.

I had over thirty films from which to select scenes. I chose those which I felt were classic Abbott & Costello routines. All the dialogue is taken directly from the soundtracks.

Wherever possible, I try to involve the subjects of my books. In the case of this volume I contacted Bud Abbott. We had one meeting in his home in California. I was shocked to find that such a strong, articulate and vibrant man was now in a wheelchair having a hard time with words. He had suffered a stroke. We spoke for a while and I explained what I was trying to do and expressed hope that I might interview him for publication in this book. He couldn't comprehend my interest in Abbott & Costello, yet as we talked he seemed to revive some of the spirit so typical of his performance. We agreed to a second meeting when I would be armed with a tape recorder. As I was leaving he pointed to a wooden structure behind his home, looked up at me and proudly said, "I've got every one of my pictures in that room back there, every one".

It has been over five months since that first meeting. We were never able to have that second meeting. Apparently a few days after our initial chat Bud Abbott fell and broke his hip. Since then he has been unable to see anyone.

RICHARD J. ANOBILE
New York City, August 1972

ACKNOWLEDGEMENTS

During the compilation of this book several people have given me a helping hand. I would like to take this opportunity to thank those people.

Initially, Herb Stern and Jim Fiedler of the Universal Law Department cleared the rights for the use of the material. Once I arrived at the studio they saw to it that anything I needed was at my disposal.

Chuck Silvers over at Universal Editorial once again did his usual terrific job and saw to it that the prints were available as well as screening rooms and editorial facilities. Chuck has involved himself with all my books and there is no doubt in my mind that he has made my job easier. In order to insure that my shirtsleeves didn't get caught up in a movieola, Chuck asked Jim Vogel, one of Universal's staff editors, to assist me in the technical end. And that he did; and I am pleased to report that I am still in one piece. Thanks, Jim.

Due to the fact that all the Abbott & Costello films are still on nitrate stock, a highly unstable material that can go up in flames quite easily under the right conditions, the films could not be brought onto the Universal lot without violating fire codes and insurance policies. Therefore all the technial work had to be carried out in New York City where facilities for handling nitrate exist.

My good friend and a fantastic editor, Sam Citron, took on the job of transferring all my marks from 16mm prints to the 35mm fine grains. He made sure I received the exact frames I had selected in California and it can go on record that he didn't miss one. Thank you, Sam.

The tremendous facilities of Movielab in New York were put into play and all the negatives were produced under the watchful eye of Fred Kovary with, I understand, a bit of harrassment from Sam. And finally, all the blowups were made at Vitaprint in New York. My thanks to everyone there.

As for the distinctive design of this book I have Harry Chester's design studio to thank, with a special mention for Alex Soma who labored long and hard over this book. Aside from bringing a talent for creative design to this book, Alex also brought a unique knowledge of the films. Thank you, Alex.

RICHARD J. ANOBILE

BUD ABBOTT AND LOU COSTELLO IN BUCK PRIVATES

In 1941, Abbott and Costello starred in their first film. It opens with Smitty (Abbott) and Herbie (Costello) doing a swift business in ties.

Smitty: I've lived on the bounty of the country. And done my boardin' with the warden.

Smitty: Never have I ever had the opportunity of presenting such merchandise. Feel that material . . that's enough. Now friends . . .

Smitty: — ordinarily this tie would sell in any haberdashery for at least a dollar and a half.

Smitty: But am I asking you for a dollar and a half? No.

Smitty: Am I asking you a dollar? No.

Smitty: Am I asking you for fifty cents? No.

Smittty: All I'm asking for is ten cents! Ah!

Smitty: Wait a minute and let me get a word in or two.

Herbie: Go ahead. Go on. I'll listen to you for a while.

Smitty: Thanks very kindly . . . now!

Smitty: Neighbor, how much have you got?

Herbie: I've got in the vicinity of twenty eight dollars.

Smitty: Oh, you got twenty eight dollars.

Herbie: In the vicinity. In the neighborhood I've got three bucks.

Smitty: Then you have three dollars?

Herbie: Roughly speaking. When you smooth it out I've got a buck.

Smitty: Then you have a dollar — you have a dollar?

Smitty: That's all I wanted to know. The gentleman buys ten ties.

Man: How can he sell ties that cheap?

Herbie: We ain't got no overhead. We ain't even got a license to sell these ties.

Smitty: Feel that tie.

Herbie: It won't wrinkle or fade — fade — f-f-f-a-a-d-e, Smitty, fade!

Smitty: What's wrong?
Herbie: The opper kay!
Smitty: Oh, oh, oh!

Cop: Come here you!

Smitty: Get in the cab.   **Herbie:** Hey, cabby!

Herbie: Step on it, we're trying to get away from the cops.

Cops: Oh yeah?

On their way to training camp, the boys get involved in a crap game. Herbie claims he's never played and Smitty is anxious to teach him.

Herbie: What are ya doin' boys?

Man: He just gave us a lesson in dice.

Herbie: What's dice?

Smitty: It's a game.

Herbie: A game?

Smitty: Don't you play games?

Herbie: Yeh, I play jacks.

Smitty: You play jacks.

Herbie: I'm up to my fourzeees.

Smitty: Oh, behave. There's the game.   **Herbie:** Will you teach me how to play that?

Smitty: Will I teach you **how** to play it — I should say I will — will I teach him?

Smitty: You see, there's numbers on there from one to six. Now you roll them out and if you should roll a one and a six — that's a seven— that's a natural — you win.

Smitty: If you roll a six and a three — that's a natural, you win.

Herbie: That's all you do is win.

Herbie: Oh you can win and ya can lose. That's fair.

Smitty: See, seven you win and craps you lose.

Herbie: Let's play.

Smitty: You wanna play? All right here ya are — you roll the dice

Herbie: Okay and we'll play for money.

Smitty: Yes and we'll play for — now how much you wanna bet?

Herbie: Ten dollars.

28

Smitty: Well — no.

Herbie: Oh — you can lose too?

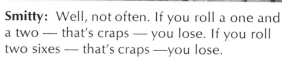

Smitty: Well, not often. If you roll a one and a two — that's craps — you lose. If you roll two sixes — that's craps —you lose.

Smitty: Ten dollars. That's a good bet. There you are. Now good luck.

Herbie: Okay — here I go —

Smitty: Seven you win and craps you lose.   Go ahead —

Herbie: Here I go —
Wheeeeee!

Herbie: Seven!
I win.

Smitty: Wait a minute, I forgot to tell you — don't pick up the money right away.

Herbie: I do get to pick it up?

Smitty: Oh, sure. It's your money.

Herbie: Yeh —

Smitty: You roll again — how much you wanna bet?

Herbie: Er-fade that.

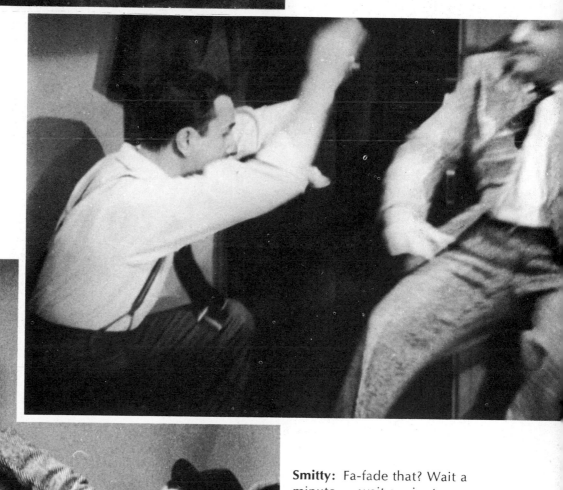

Smitty: Fa-fade that? Wait a minute — wait a minute — just a minute — just a minute here —

Herbie: Don't get so rough.

Smitty: Wait a minute — where did you get that 'fade that?'

Herbie: Why, did I say something wrong?

Smitty: No — you said it too darn right.

Smitty: Sorry — you sure you never played this game before? All right.

Smitty: There you are — go ahead.

Herbie: Same thing?

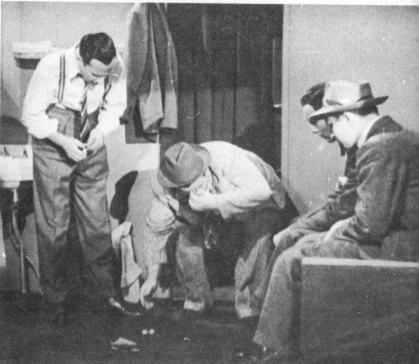

Smitty: Yeh, same thing. Go ahead.

Herbie: There I go again — whee!

Herbie: Did it again. I win.

Smitty: Yes, you win again. Well, I guess it's beginners luck.

Smitty: All right. Now what do you want to bet now.

Herbie: Let 'er ride.

Smitty: Now, wait a minute. Don't tell me you got that out of thin air?

Herbie: I got that at the clubhouse.

Smitty: That's what I thought.

Herbie: I must confess.

Smitty: Come on.

Smitty: Let it ride? Now just a minute . . .

Herbie: Well, there was a bunch of boys over at the clubhouse and they had lumps of sugar; they were throwing them out and I heard one of the boys say that.

Smitty: But you didn't play in the game?

Herbie: They didn't let me. I was too young.

Smitty: Oh, that's different.

Herbie: Startin' Tuesday, I'm going out with girls.

Smitty: Well, I don't blame you. Why that's all right. I thought you played the game. Same thing?

Herbie: Same thing . . . whoooo!

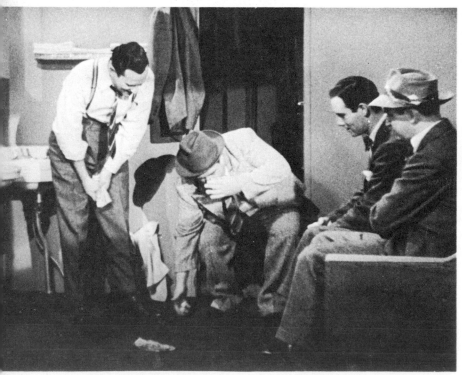

Smitty: There you are, four.

Herbie: A little Joe!

Smitty: A little Joe. Now wait a minute, now just a minute, just a minute.

Herbie: Club house — club house!

Smitty: Club house — yeah. You learned an awful lot at that club house. Four is your number. Don't forget, if you throw a seven before you make that four you lose.

Herbie: Okay.

Smitty: Go ahead.

Smitty: Uh-uh-uh-uh-uh.

Herbie: I'll be legitimate.

Smitty: Yeah, you better be.

Herbie: Club house.

Smitty: um-hum, club house.

Herbie: Three!

Smitty: I said seven loses.

Herbie: Oh, you add them up? You didn't say anything about adding them up.

Smitty: You lose.

Herbie: How come.

Smitty: Well what did you roll the first time?

Herbie: Four.

Smitty: What did you just roll?

Herbie: Three

Smitty: Four and three is what?

Herbie: Seven.

Smitty: Go down to the clubhouse and learn that.

Herbie: That ain't fair.

Smitty: Now wait a minute, now wait a minute. We'll play my way now.

Herbie: You mean I gotta use my money now?

Smitty: For a change, yes. You used mine long enough. Put it all down.

Smitty: You don't care, do you? Now watch it — here they go!

Herbie: Six.

Smitty: Six is the point. Well, boys, watch this one, six again.

Herbie: You lose.

Smitty: No, no, no, no, no! I win.

Herbie: What did you roll the first time?

Smitty: Six.

Herbie: What did you just roll?

Smitty: Six.

Herbie: Six and six are twelve. Six — twelve — craps, box cars, big bennys!

Smitty rearranges Herbie's finances.

Smitty: Hi ya, neighbor — how ya feller?   **Herbie:** Not a penny.

Smitty: Oh come — come — I didn't ask you for any money.

Herbie: You've got that look in your eye.

Smitty: Now listen — you cleaned me up in that crap game, didn't you?

Herbie: You gave me a lesson — that's all I know.

Smitty: Oh do me a favor — loan me fifty bucks.

Herbie: Smitty, I can't — I can't lend you fifty dollars.

Smitty: Oh, yes you can.

Herbie: No I can't. All I got is forty dollars.

Smitty: All right, give me the forty dollars. And you owe me ten —

Herbie: Okay I owe you ten.

Smitty: All right.

Herbie: How come I owe you ten?

Smitty: What did I ask you for?

Herbie: Fifty dollars.

Smitty: And how much did you give me?

Herbie: Forty dollars.

Smitty: So? You owe me ten dollars.

Herbie: That's right. But you owe me forty.

Smitty: Now don't change the subject.

Herbie: I'm not changing the subject.

Herbie: You're trying to change my finances. Give me my forty dollars.

Smitty: All right now there's your forty dollars. Now give me the ten dollars you owe me.

Smitty: That's the way you feel about it, that's the last time I'll ever ask you for the loan of fifty dollars.

Herbie: Wait a minute, Smitty. How can I loan you fifty dollars now. All I have is thirty.

Herbie: I'm paying you on account.

Smitty: On account?

Herbie: Yeh, on account of I don't know how I owe it to you.

Smitty: Well, give me the thirty and you'll owe me the twenty.

Herbie: Okay — this is getting worse all the time. First you owe me ten and now I owe another twenty.

Smitty: Why do you run yourself into debt?

Herbie: I'm not running in — you're pushin 'me.

Smitty: I can't help it if you can't handle your finances. I do all right with my money.

Herbie: I was doing all right with mine too.

Smitty: All right, here's your 30 dollars. Now give me back the 20 you owe me.

Smitty: You're a fine guy. Won't loan a pal 50 dollars.

Smitty: Now I asked you for the loan of fifty dollars and you gave me thirty so you owe me twenty dollars. 20 and 30 is fifty.

Herbie: No-no-oh no — 25 and 25 is 50.

Herbie: How can I loan you 50? All I got now is 10.
Smitty: Listen, to show you I'm your pal, you want to double that?
Herbie: Go ahead. I'll see you later.

Smitty: Say, listen, I don't want that kind of money. On the up and up — hold it. Now take a number. Any number at all from 1 to 10 and don't tell me.

Herbie: I got it.

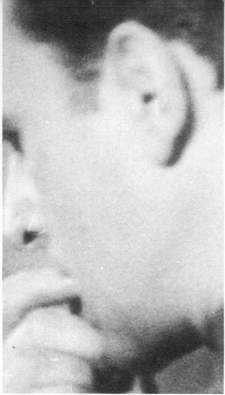

Smitty: Is the number odd or even?

Herbie: Even.

Herbie: No. I think I got him.

Smitty: Is it between 5 and 7?

Herbie: Yeah.

Smitty: Is the number between 1 and 3?

Herbie: No.

Smitty: Between 3 and 5?

Smitty: Number 6.

Herbie: Right!

Herbie: How did he do that?

Smitty asks the question and Herbie tries to answer.

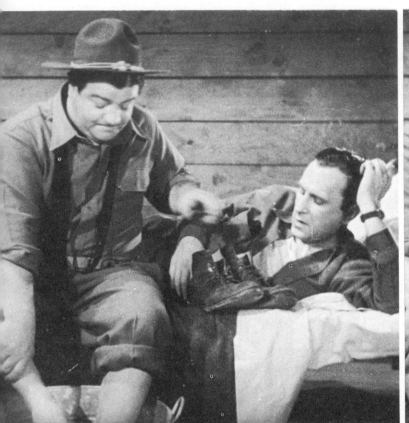 

Smitty: Answer this question. You're forty years old and you're in love with a little girl who's ten years old —

Herbie: This one's gonna be a pip.

Smitty: Well, wait until I finish.

Herbie: — me, running around with a ten year old girl!

Smitty: Well, wait a minute.

Herbie: You might get a good idea where I'm gonna wind up.

Smitty: Will you wait a minute. You're forty years old and you're in love wtih this little girl that's ten years old. You're four times as old as that girl and you can't marry her. Could you?

Herbie: Not unless I come from the mountains.

Smitty: All right, all right —

Herbie: Why don't you ask me something this big.

Smitty: Wait, wait until I finish this.

56

Smitty: You're forty years old, you're four times as old as this girl, — and you can't marry her so you wait five years.

Smitty: By that time the little girl's fifteen and you're forty-five.

Smitty: You're only three times as old as that little girl. So wait fifteen years more and when the girl is thirty you're sixty.

Smitty: You're only twice as old as that little girl.

Herbie: She's catching up.

Smitty: Yes, yes. Now here's the question. How long do you have to wait until you and that little girl are the same age?

Herbie: Well, what kind of a question is that? That's ridiculous.

Smitty: Ridiculous or not — Answer the question.

Herbie: If I wait for that girl she'll pass me up. She'll wind up older than I am.

Smitty: What are you talking about?
Herbie: She'll have to wait for me.
Smitty: Why should she wait for you?

Herbie: . I was nice enough to wait for her.

Smitty: Aw, go to bed.

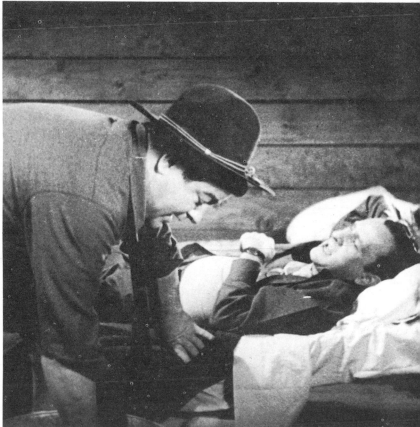

Herbie: If that little girl don't want to marry me, she don't have to marry me.

Smitty: Aw, you're silly, you're silly.

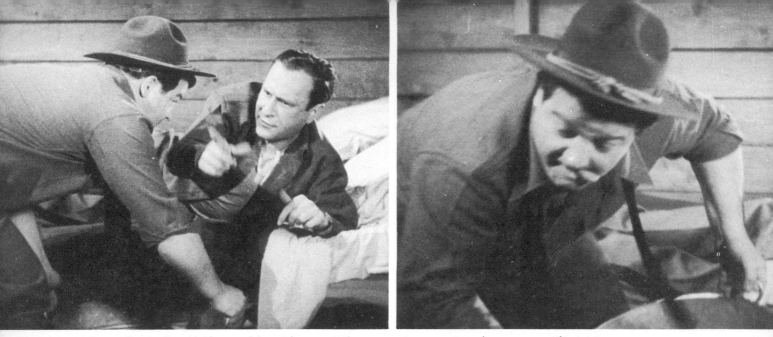

Smitty: That's the whole trouble with you. Where are you putting that water. Throw it out.

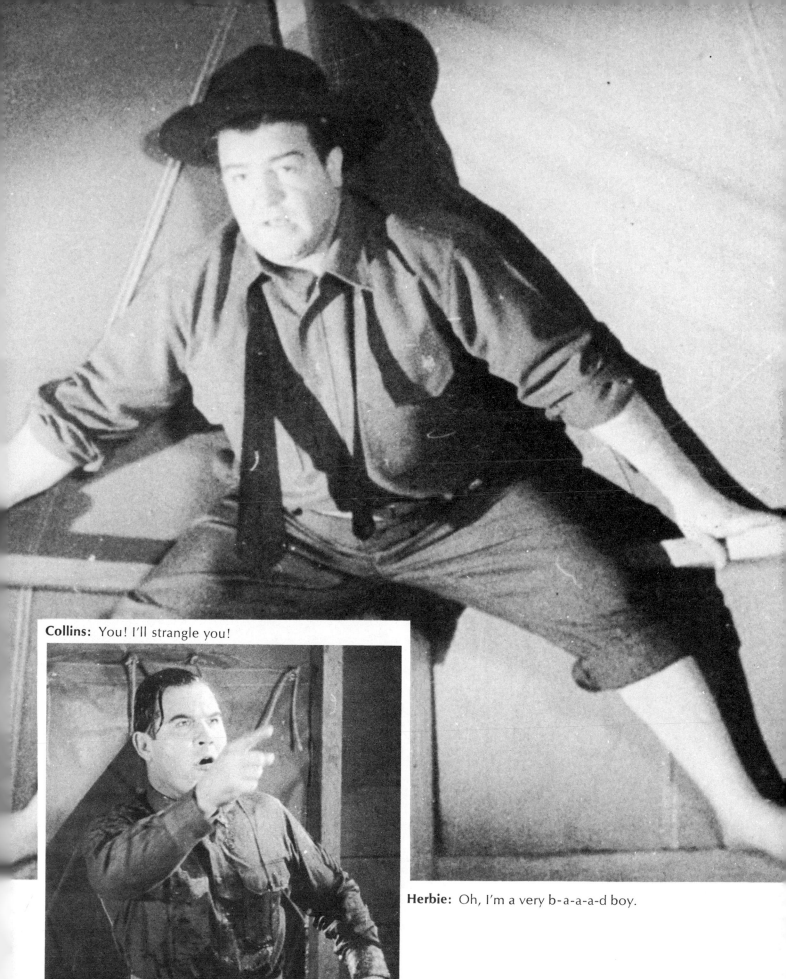

Collins: You! I'll strangle you!

Herbie: Oh, I'm a very b-a-a-a-d boy.

UNIVERSAL-INTERNATIONAL
PRESENTS

Bud
Abbott

Lou
Costello

IN

Buck Privates
Come Home

**Herbie (Costello)
decides to even a score.**

1st Soldier: Say, what comes after this medical examination?
2nd Soldier: You're a civilian, Bud.
Steve: What's a civilian?
Slicker: That's a guy that tells you about the great times he had when he was in the Army.

Herbie: Yeah! When they get you in the Army they rush you to bed, and then they rush you to get up. They rush you here — they rush you there — they rush you everywhere. And when it's time for you to get out everybody takes their time.
Collins: Stop gripin'

63

Herbie: Stop gripin'! Sergeant, you and me got a score to settle. When you were a cop, if I hit you it was resisting an officer. And if I hit you when you are a Sergeant it's insubordination. But when you and me go out that front gate we're civilians.

Collins: Then what?

Herbie: I'll forget about the whole thing.

Collins: Bah!

Herbie: I guess I scared him.

After discharge, Herbie and Slicker (Abbott) go right back into the tie business.

Slicker: Step right up. Today, and today only, I am selling fifteen dollar ties for thirty-five cents. Think of it, gentlemen! Pure silk and wears like iron. I hope! My merchandise speaks for itself. Far be it from me to resort to the power of suggestion, but I —

Slicker: Now, if some kind gentleman would step forward. It only takes a second. Anyone at all!

Herbie: Thank you — and thank you.

Slicker: Wait I'll show you one better. I will demonstrate, gentlemen. Of course I will need a subject.

Slicker: Would you step forward?
Herbie: Hello!

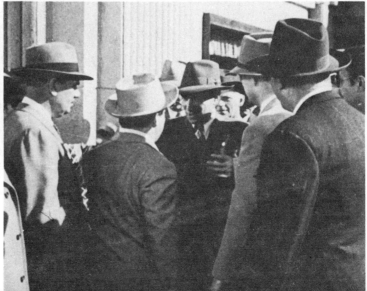

Slicker: Thank you stranger for stepping up.
Herbie: Stranger?! Why, Slicker.

Slicker: Yes, yes. Just a minute. Everything's going to be all right.

Slicker: Now, gentlemen, I — want to prove to you that I can hypnotize each and every one of you and sell you my ties. But far be it from me to do anything dishonest.

Slicker: Now just keep your eyes on me gentlemen. Now uh — just look into my eyes. Now just stand still. I'm going to put you to sleep.

Herbie: Going to put me to sleep?
Slicker: Yes.
Herbie: I just got up.
Slicker: That's quite all right. I'm going to put you to sleep.
Herbie: Going to be a short day.

Slicker: All right now. Just look into my eyes. Look into my eyes. There you are. You tell me when you get sleepy. Tell me when you get drowsy.
Herbie: When I get what?
Slicker: Drowsy! Drowsy!
Herbie: Oh.

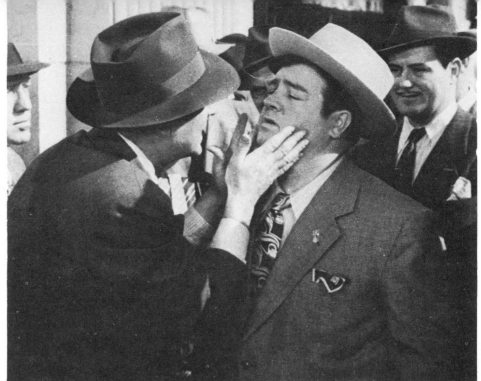

Slicker: Now take it easy now.
Herbie: Drowsy.

Slicker: All right. All right. Please. Pay attention to the Professor.

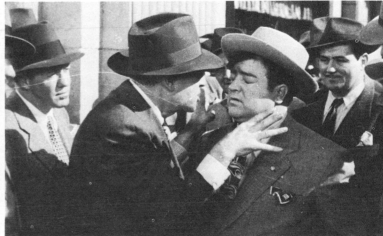

Slicker: There you are. Stand still. There we are. There we are.

Herbie: Look. Now you have to — I mean that's not nice. Now put me to sleep but don't go — but that — that — that's not nice.

Slicker: Say, will you stand still please? Now just hold still a minute.

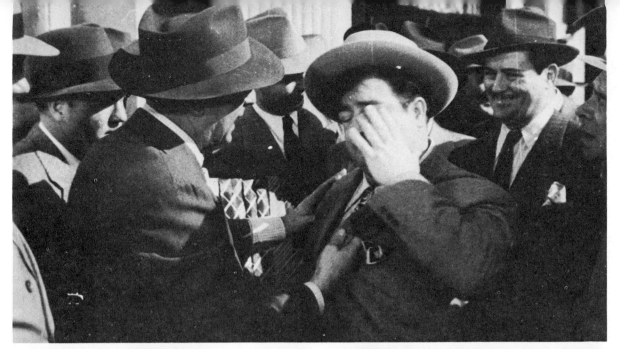

Herbie: There he goes again, spitt'in.

Slicker: Will you stand still, please?
Herbie: That's not nice — in the face like that. I mean, because after all. I don't go for that — now — now — now don't do it again.
Slicker: Will you do as I tell you? Stand still.
Herbie: Sell the ties nice, but don't — don't go like that because —

Slicker: Just a minute, please. Where do you think you're at? What's the matter with you?

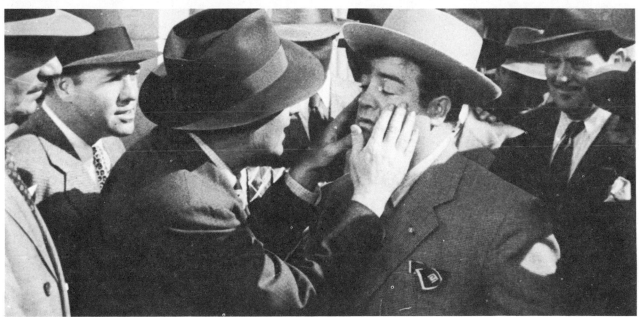

Slicker: Quiet. There, he's going. There he's going. There you are, boys. The boy's now in a state of coma. Cannot utter a word. Am I right?

Herbie: Right.   **Slicker:** Right.

Slicker: Now gentlemen, I want to prove to you these ties are absolutely wrinkle proof.

Slicker: You see I have here three ties securely knotted together. Feel that knot. Feel that. That's the idea. Now boys — I'm going to take uh — here, loan me your hat a minute.

Herbie: What for?
Slicker: I want to do a trick in it.
Herbie: Not my hat.

Slicker: Oh, come, come, come. Just hold on to it. I'm not going to harm your hat, my friend.

Slicker: I'm going to throw these ties, securely knotted, into the hat. Like that. Now friends, if anyone of those ties come out of that hat with a wrinkle in it, I'll make you a present of it. Watch it. Hocus pocus alacazam.

Slicker: And here we have tie number one.

Slicker: Here we have tie number two.

Slicker: And here we have tie number three.

Slicker: Without a wrinkle in 'em, —

Man: I'll take three ties.
Slicker: Now you're talking, sir.

Herbie: Hey. What am I going to do with these?

a short take...

Herbie: I'd rather marry a homely girl than a pretty girl anyway.
Slicker: Why?
Herbie: Well, if you marry a pretty girl she's liable to run away.

Evey: But, Uncle Herbie, isn't a homely girl liable to run away too?

Herbie: Yeah, but who cares?

Herbie (Sings):
We're goin' to bed
We're goin' to bed
Oh, tonight's the first night I'll really
    get some sleep.

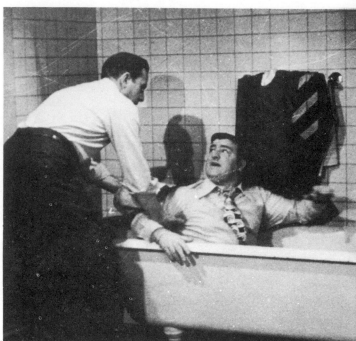

Slicker: Oh, wait a minute. Wait a minute.
Wait a minute.
Herbie: Thank you, Slicker. Thank you.

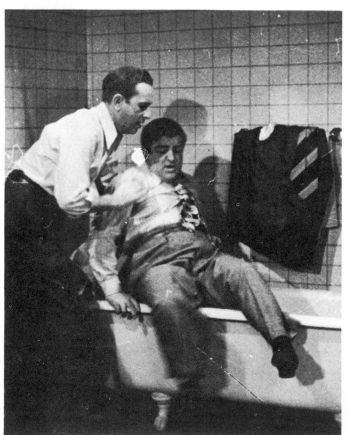

Slicker: Get up out of there! Get up! I'm
sleepin' there!

Herbie: Well, you just put me in, didn't you?
Slicker: Don't give me that!

Herbie: You put me in like a little baby. Like a mama puts a little baby to bed.

Slicker: That's my bed!
Herbie: I was already in it!

Slicker: You'll stay out of it!
Herbie: That's no way to treat a returned veteran!

Slicker: Aw, go away! What's the matter? Returned veteran! When we were overseas, you didn't fire off a gun!

Herbie: I didn't have to. I did all my fightin' with a knife!
Slicker: With a knife?
Herbie: With a knife. I had six thousand, three hundred and eighty-two to my credit.
Slicker: Enemies?
Herbie: No. Potatoes.

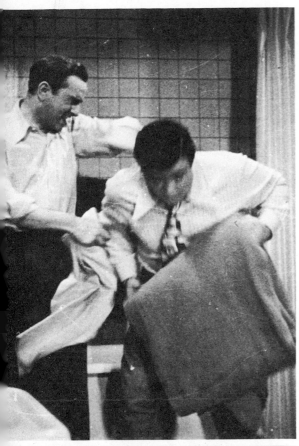

Slicker: Oh, stop!
Herbie: And furthermore, I was right where the bullets were the thickest.
Slicker: Where was that?

Herbie: Underneath the ammunition truck.

Smokey (Abbott) and Pomeroy (Costello) come into town to deliver a letter for the Captain.

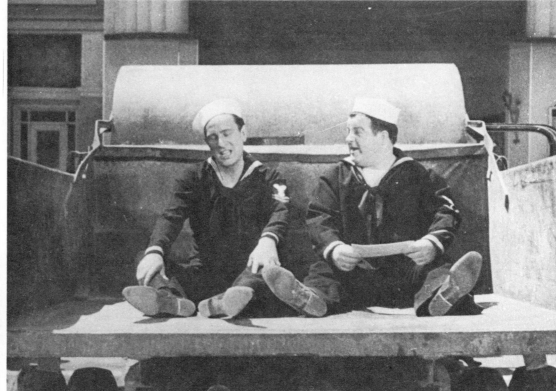

Driver: Where do you gobs want off?

Smokey: Just dump us off any where.

Driver: Okay, buddies.

Pomeroy: Whee! Thanks a lot.

Smokey: Come here.

Smokey: There. Have you still got the letter?

Pomeroy: Sure I got the letter. Mr. Thomas Halstead . . . . Conquistador Hotel. This guy must be a big shot if the Captain sends him private messages.

Smokey: I still can't understand why the Captain sent you to deliver that message.

Pomeroy: Because I'm the smartest man in the navy.

Smokey: How do you figure that?

Pomeroy: He said it was impossible for anybody to teach me anything.

After creating a monumental traffic jam, Smokey and Pomeroy are collared by a policeman and the shore patrol.

Pomeroy: What's the matter with you guys? Ain't you got any sense? You want to hurt somebody? You wouldn't drive like that if there was a cop around here.

Smokey: Yeah.

Pomeroy: How do you like that? There ain't a cop within a mile here. Nobody would ever drive like that . . . you go call me a policeman.

Cop: Sure . . . . what?

Smokey: Hush, hush.

Dynamite: Say, didn't you sailors hear that officer blow his whistle?

Smokey: Yes.

Dynamite: Well, what do you think he's doing? Giving bird imitations or does he look like a peanut stand?

Cop: Say, don't you know there's a law in this town against jay walking.

Smokey: He knows it. Give him a ticket.

85

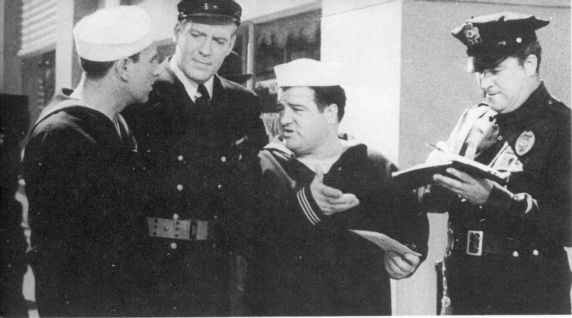

Pomeroy: Now wait a minute, Smokey.

Smokey: You keep out of this.

Pomeroy: Don't tell the man to give me a ticket.

Smokey: I'll get you out of this. What are you worrying about?

Pomeroy: You'll get me out of this? In a patrol wagon?

Cop: I don't like to give a sailor a ticket.

Pomeroy: See, he don't want to give a sailor a ticket.

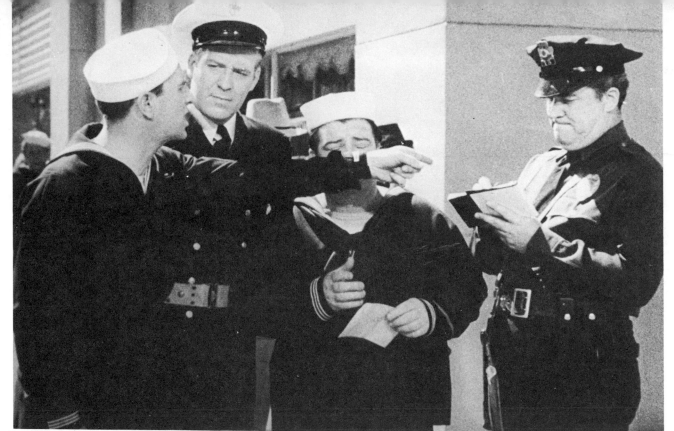

Smokey: It's your duty. Give him a ticket.

Pomeroy: But Smokey, why can't you leave the man alone?

Smokey: You keep quiet. I insist that you give him a ticket.

Pomeroy: He's a persistent sort of a guy. He says for you to give me a ticket.

Smokey: You just keep quiet. He can't bluff me.

Dynamite: Go ahead. Give him one.

Cop: Okay, if you insist. What's your name?

Pomeroy: Pomeroy Watson.

Dynamite: What ship?

Pomeroy: No ship. I ain't never been on a boat.

Dynamite: What?

Pomeroy: I only been in the navy six years.

Cop: Never been to sea?

Pomeroy: No, sir? Revolting, isn't it.

Dynamite: Next time watch your step — both of you.

Pomeroy — My first ticket, and I wasn't even driving a car. See what you got me?

Smokey: Wait a minute.

Pomeroy: See what I got to get on account of you people?

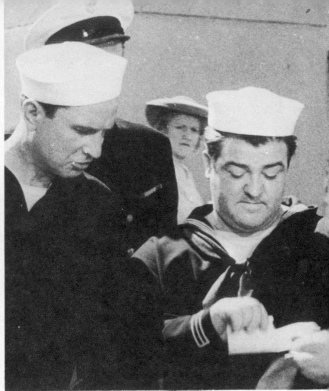

Smokey: Wait a minute, wait a minute. He can't bluff you. Tear it up.

Pomeroy: It's no good, ain't it?

Smokey: Tear it up! Go on. He can't do anything to you.

Pomeroy: Okay.

Dynamite: Hey, What's the idea?

Pomeroy: It was his idea.

Dynamite: Yeah? Tell that to the Marines.

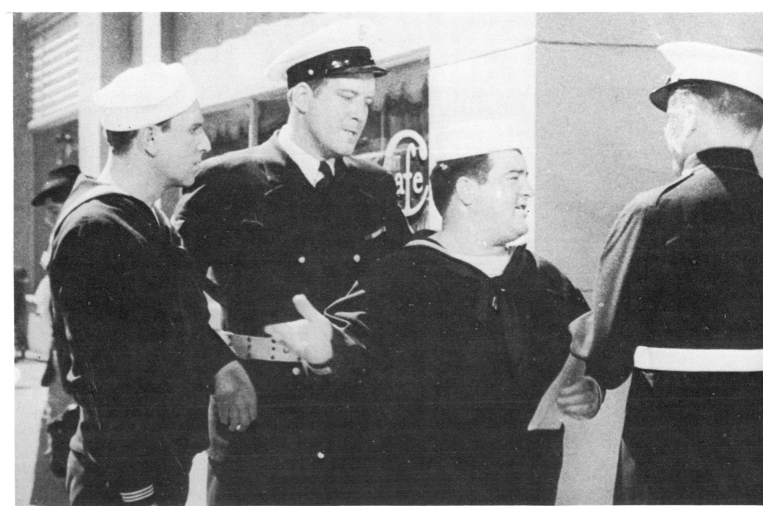

Pomeroy: It was his idea. I was — I got a ticket here —

The object of the game is to find the lemon. This is a good example of pure Abbott and Costello. Keep your eye on that lemon — and on the basket under the table.

Smokey: Oh, where'd you get all that? Well, I didn't know you had all that money.

Pomeroy: Oh sure.

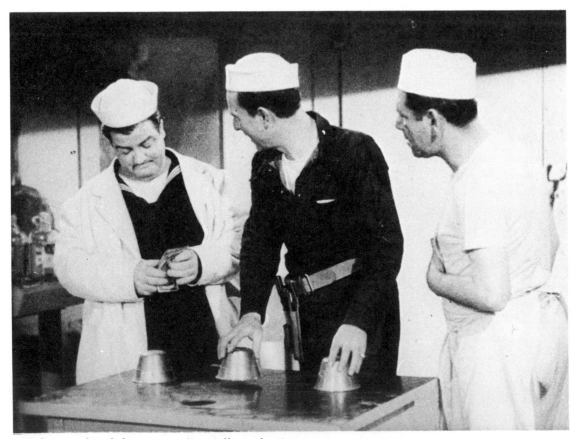

Smokey: Why didn't you tell a fellow that?

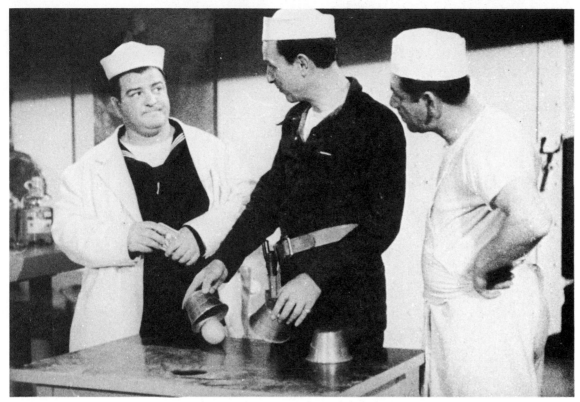

Pomeroy: You've got a certain look in your eye that I don't like.

Smokey: Oh, behave — I'm your friend.

Pomeroy: What are you doing?

Smokey: Oh, it's a little game. A little game called "Find the submarine" — Do you like to play games?

Smokey: Well, you see, that's a submarine.

Pomeroy: That's a lemon.

Smokey: Well, we call it a submarine.

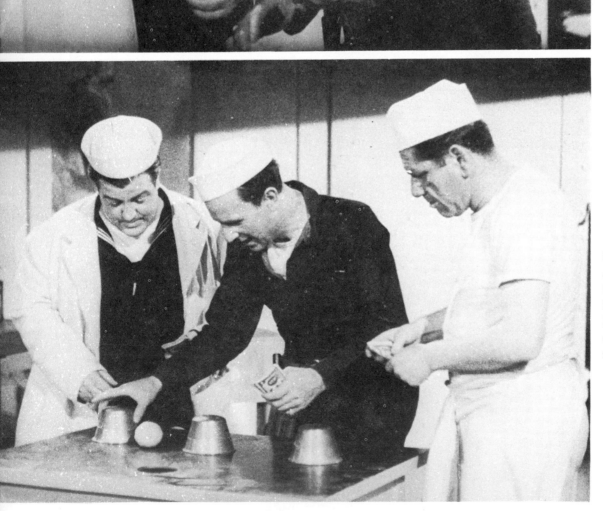

Smokey: Well that's the Atlantic Ocean — that's the Pacific Ocean and that's the Indian Ocean. I place it in one of the oceans — you find the submarine and you win.

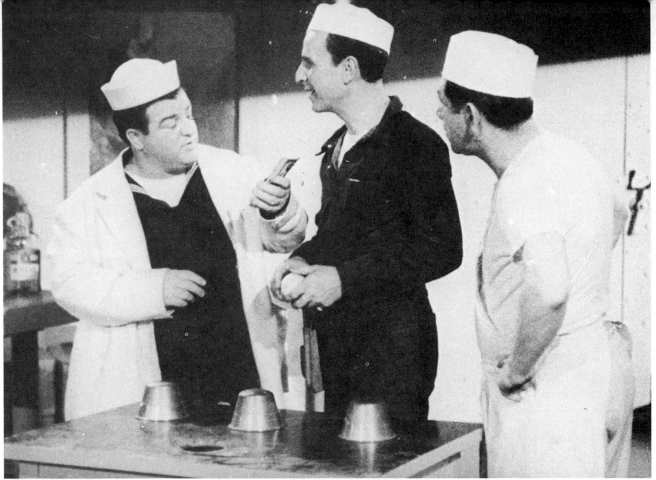

Pomeroy: Oh then that's different. Then we'll play. Get your money up — let's play.

Smokey: All right — You got the idea of the game. All right, now watch it — see it there? Now you know we put it in the Pacific Ocean.

Smokey: Keep your eye on it. Tell me where it is.

Pomeroy: I pick this one over here.

Smokey: Keep your eye on it. Tell me where it is.

Pomeroy: I pick this one over here. I'll play Ten Dollars.

Smokey: Ten Dollars for me — Ten Dollars for you —

Smokey: Well, it wasn't there. Can you imagine that? It wasn't there. I can't help it.

Pomeroy: Somehow it got away fast.

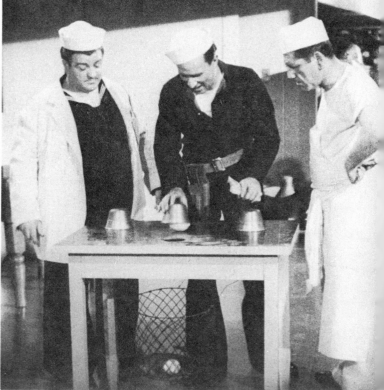

Smokey: Too bad — well they do that, you know.

Pomeroy: Give me another chance.

Smokey: All right — here you are.

Smokey: No, not under there.

Dizzy: Not under there — it wasn't there.

Pomeroy: I could swear it was under there.

Smokey: You see it there — how can you go wrong? It's just a little twist of the wrist. There she goes.

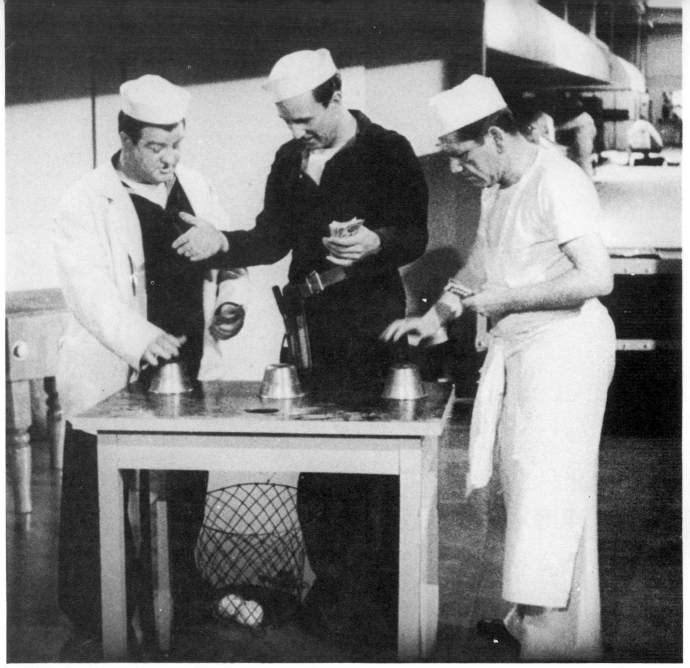

Smokey: Where she is nobody knows.

Pomeroy: I'll take this one for Ten Dollars.

Smokey: Ten Dollars for you.

Pomeroy: Come over here.

Smokey: Come on. That's it — now you've got it.

Pomeroy: Come on — come on.

Smokey: Wait a minute, put it down once, you know.

Pomeroy: O. K.

Smokey: Where is it? It wasn't there and it wasn't there.

Pomeroy: I don't figure anybody can win in this game, Smokey.

Smokey: I don't say that.

Pomeroy: I sure said it.

Smokey: There it is — right there. Now if I can find it, why can't you.

Pomeroy: What kind of a bet is that? Go ahead — betcha Ten Dollars and it's right there and you pick it up yourself.

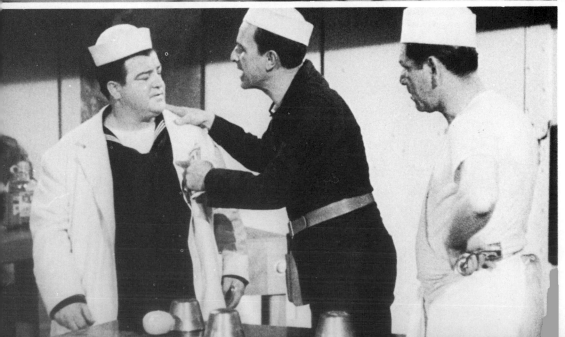

Smokey: Listen, I'll give you a chance again. Look, for One Dollar.

Pomeroy: There — on the other side, the ones.

Smokey: One Dollar. Now you find it.

Pomeroy: Okay.

Smokey: Now, you win, so we're even all right.

Pomeroy: What d'ya start betting dollars for now? You've been betting Tens right along.

Smokey: Well then I'll give you a chance to double up on me. Here, you see it there?

Pomeroy: Go ahead.

Smokey: Now, watch — watch it. Now it's underneath one of those shells.

Pomeroy: Ten Dollars — under here.

Smokey: You can't — yeh, go ahead. Did you find it? Now if he can find it — why can't you? Now, Dizzy if you want to make a little bet on the side —

Pomeroy: Ten Dollars it's under here.   **Smokey:** Now go ahead — pick it out — It's up to you.

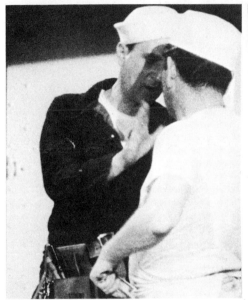  

Smokey: Now if he wins then, then —   **Pomeroy:** Ten Dollars for me — Ten Dollars.   **Dizzy:** I'll take a chance.

Smokey: Go ahead — why shouldn't you?

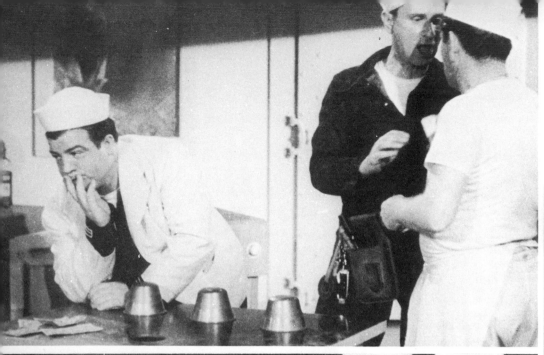

Smokey: Well, figure it out — where is it?

Smokey: Go on, pick it out.

Pomeroy: Why don't you leave them alone?

Pomeroy: There it is — no.

Dizzy: It's here. **Smokey:** He says it's there.

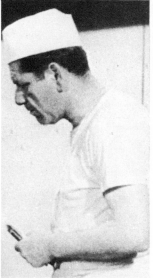

Pomeroy: There it is. **Dizzy:** I win. I win. The first time I ever won in my life.

Smokey: Well, what do you win? You've got no money down. Now the chances are if you had some money down there — the chances are you'd have won.

Dizzy: Chances are I would have lost.

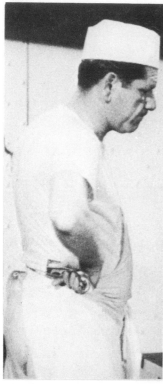

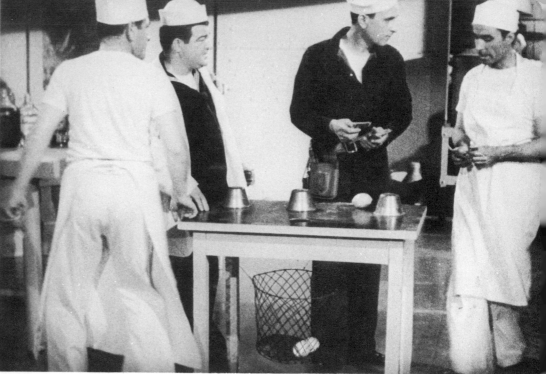

Joe: Hey, Smokey . . . I bet I could win at that submarine game.

Smokey: Okay, how much do you want to bet?

Joe: Five dollars.

Smokey: Five dollars.

Smokey: Say, have you got a ten dollar bill for some ones?

Pomeroy: Certainly. I always carry a ten dollar bill.

Smokey: That's fine.

Pomeroy: Give me the ones.

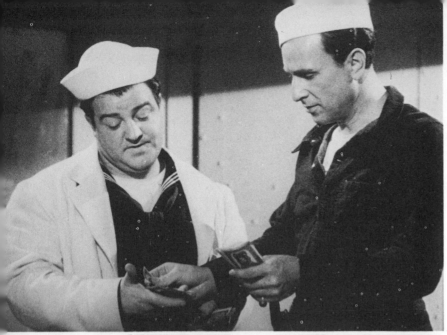

Smokey: Well, there's one — two — by the way, how many years have you been in the navy?

Pomeroy: Six years.

Smokey: *Six.*

Pomeroy: What's that got to do with counting out my change?

Smokey: *Six.*

Pomeroy: Yes.

Smokey: Seven - eight - nine - ten.

Pomeroy: That's much better.

Pomeroy: There's something wrong. You didn't give me no ten ones that time.

Smokey: Okay, here's your ten.

Pomeroy: You won't cheat me, you bet.

Smokey: Here's your ten, give me back the ones.

Pomeroy: That's better.

Smokey: Come on, come on.

Pomeroy: Okay. Now here . . . one — two . . . three . . four . . . five . . .

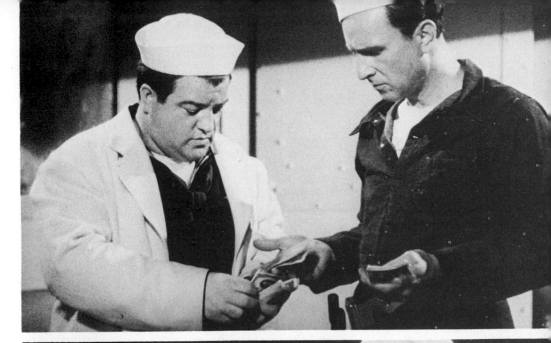

Smokey: Wait a minute. When do you get out of the navy?

Pomeroy: In two years.

Smokey: Two.

Pomeroy: Two. In two years I get out.

Smokey: Two.

Pomeroy: Two . . . three . . . four . . . five . . . six . . . seven . . .

Smokey: Wait a minute — did I understand you to say six?

Pomeroy: Six years I've been in the navy.

Smokey: Oh that's what it was.

Pomeroy: In two years I'm getting out.

Smokey: Well, I had that six on my mind. It's two years?

Pomeroy: Don't get me mixed up. That's all. I get out in two years.

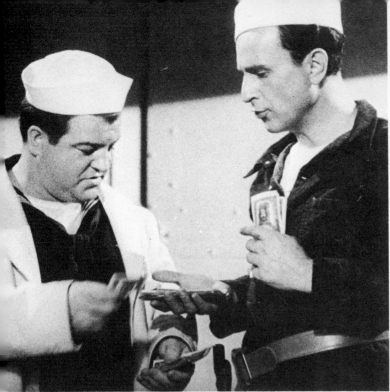

Smokey: Two, two.

Pomeroy: Two, two.

Smokey: Okay, two —

Pomeroy: three . . . four
. . . five . . six . . . seven . . . eight
. . . nine . . . ten . . .

Smokey: Thanks.

Pomeroy: I got it again.

Pomeroy: Hey, Dizzy, have you got a ten for some ones?

Dizzy: Yeah.

Pomeroy: Give me the ten. There's one . . . two . . .

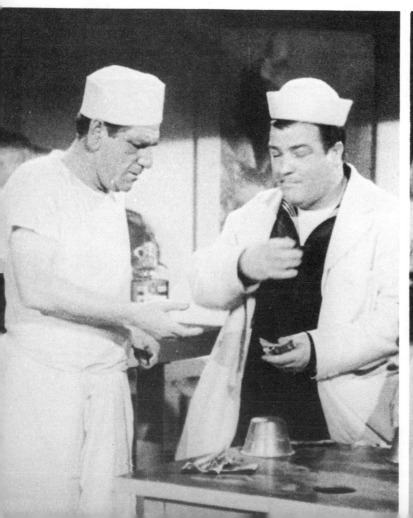

Pomeroy: How long have you been in the navy?

Dizzy: Ninety days. Come on, count it out.

Pomeroy: No, you count it. How long have you been in the navy?

Dizzy: Ninety days.

Pomeroy: It's not going to come out . . . something's wrong.

Smokey: Something you got yourself into.

Dizzy: Come on. Count it out.

Pomeroy: I'm going to get it again. Two, three, four, five, six, seven, seven. How many months in ninety days?

Dizzy: Three months.

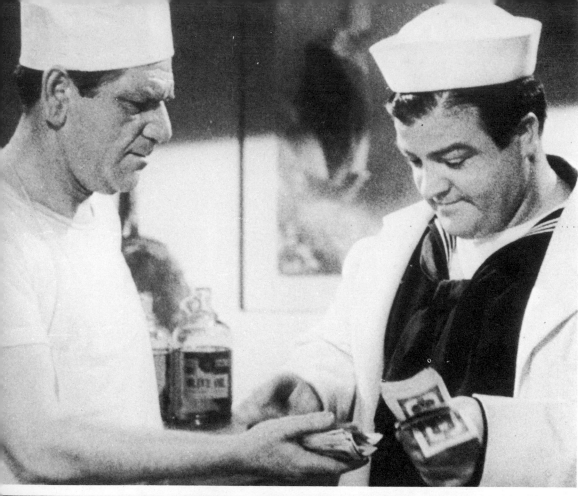

Pomeroy: Three months? Three. Three months. Three. I got it.

Dizzy: What?

Pomeroy: Three, four, five, six, seven, eight, nine, ten.

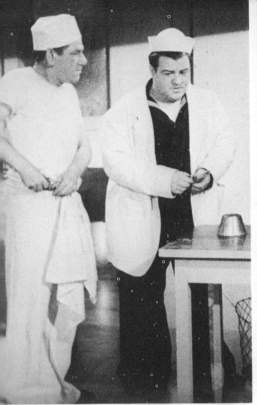

Pomeroy: I think I got it again.

Smokey: Come on! Give Joe a chance to win some money, will you please. Now look, Joe, You see it there? How can you go wrong?

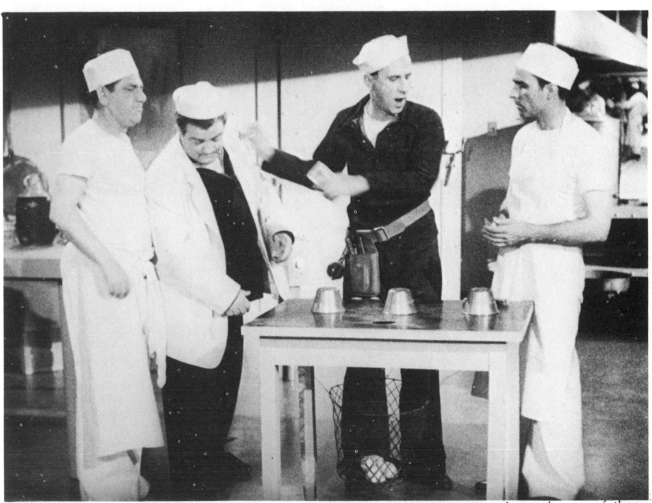

Smokey: It's just a little twist of the wrist. That's all there is to it. Now it's underneath one of those shells.

Pomeroy: Dizzy! Look under the table. Under the table! You're a cheat.

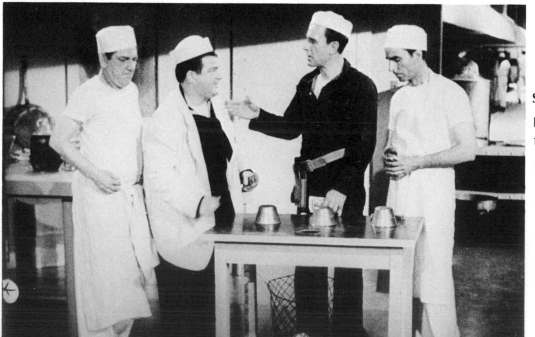

Smokey: No remarks.

Pomeroy: He's got a fruitstand under the table.

Smokey: Keep quiet.

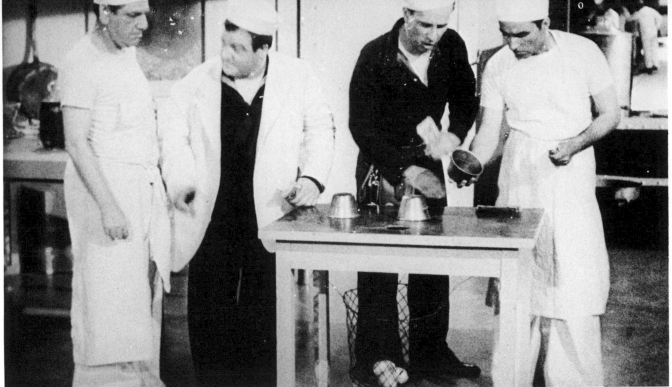

Smokey: Pick — pick it out. Go ahead
Where's the submarine? No. It wasn't there.

Joe: It's a gyp.

Smokey: What do you call a gyp? Now, just
a minute, Joe.

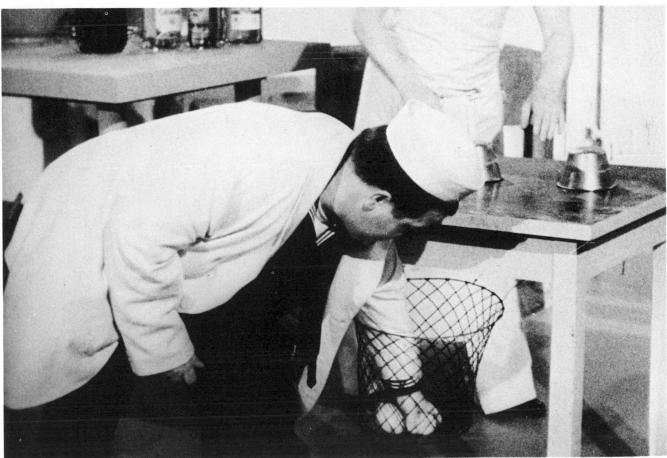

Joe: It's a gyp, I tell you.

Smokey: Now Joe — all right. Here's your money back.

Pomeroy: Trying to cheat his old friends.

Pomeroy: We ain't gonna fight —- we ain't gonna fight. I want to play some more with you, brother.

Smokey: Play some more?

Pomeroy: You ain't gonna cheat me. Give me another chance.

Smokey: Dizzy, have you got any more money?

Dizzy: Why, certainly, I've got a bankroll. What odds will you give me?

Smokey: I'll give you two to one.

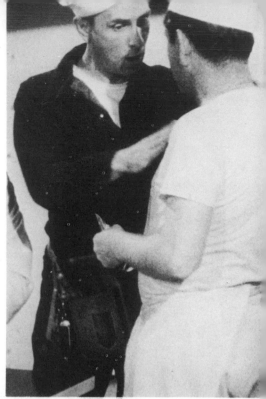

Dizzy: That ain't enough.

Smokey: Come on! I'll give you three to one.

Dizzy: You're too anxious. At least — six.

Smokey: I'll give you five to one.

Dizzy: No, six.

Smokey: I'll give you six to one.

Dizzy: Okay.

Smokey: What was that?

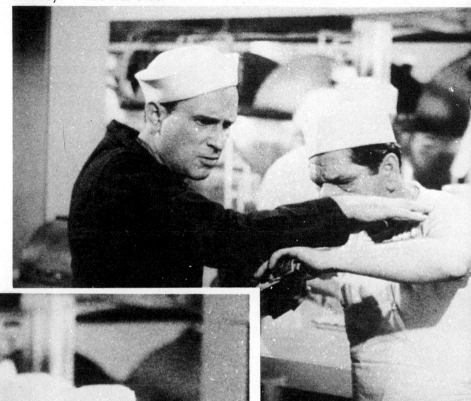

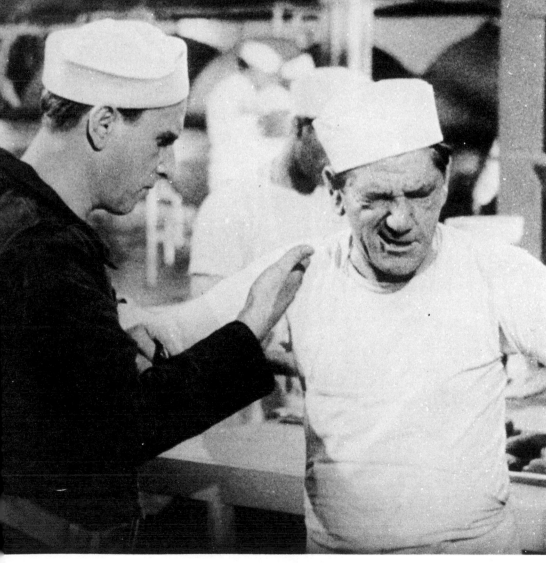

Dizzy: I don't know. Somebody is digging clams or something.

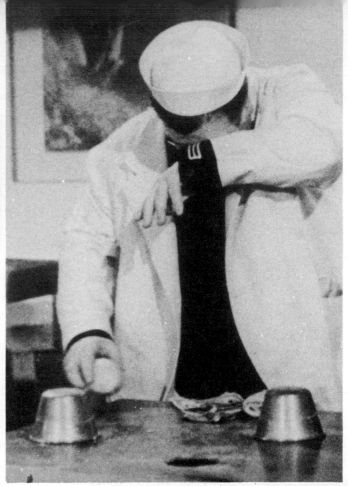

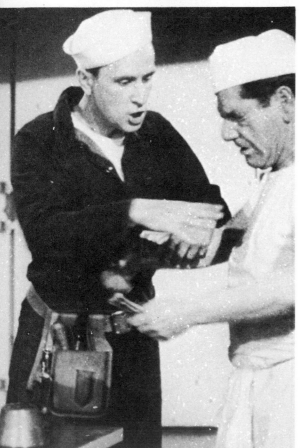

Smokey: All right. I'll tell you what we'll do. You know where it is now.

Dizzy: Yes.

Smokey: You know where the submarine is?

Dizzy: Yes.

Smokey: Well, the bank roll. All right now. Pick it up.

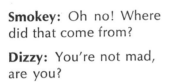

Smokey: Oh no! Where did that come from?

Dizzy: You're not mad, are you?

Smokey: Certainly I'm mad.

Dizzy: Then suck the lemon.

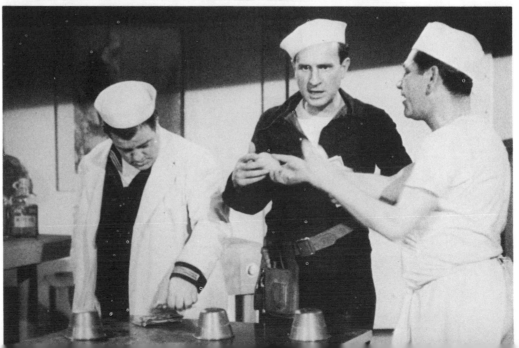

Pomeroy: Ooooh! That's the worst thing I ever saw — cheating like that. I never saw anything like it.

Smokey: Imagine a man doing that to me.

Pomeroy: One thing I never do is cheat.

Smokey: You— you know where the submarine is?

Pomeroy: I know where a whole flock of submarines are.

Smokey: For how much?

Pomeroy: I know where a submarine with juice coming out of it is.

Smokey: *How much?*

Pomeroy: The bank roll.

Smokey: You want to bet it all?

Pomeroy: The whole works.

Smokey: All right. Of course, you're only entitled to one ocean.

Pomeroy: That's all I want.

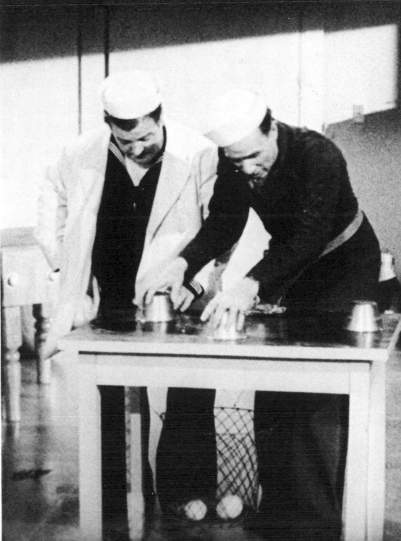

Smokey: You pick out the ocean.

Pomeroy: I'll pick up the ocean.

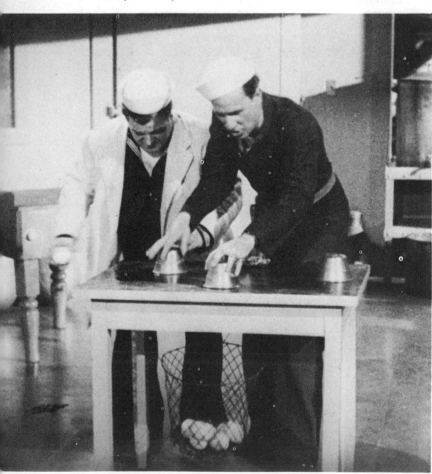

Smokey: See that ocean there? You've got to pick it up in order to win you know.

Pomeroy: Let me stay still.

Smokey: You've got to uncover the submarine.

Smokey: What ocean do you want? Come on — What's under this?

Pomeroy: That must be a triple-barrelled sub-marine. Hey, Dizzy! Look! Come here!

Pomeroy applies the new math to baking.

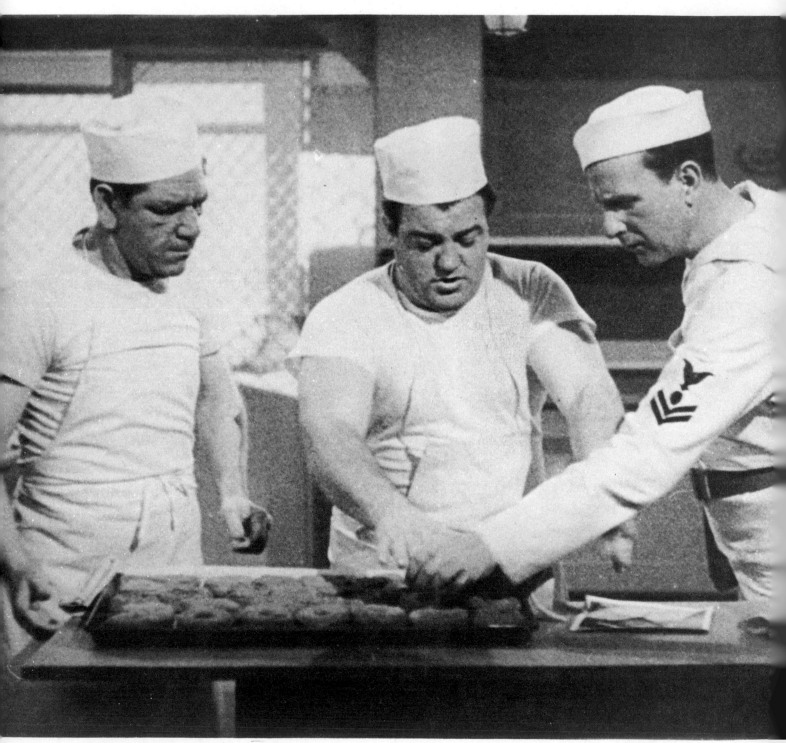

Pomeroy: Don't. I haven't got enough.

Pomeroy: I just baked 28 of these things. I mean, after all, there's 7 officers I've got to feed and I have just enough to give them 13 apiece.

Smokey: You've got what —??

Pomeroy: 13 apiece.

Smokey: 13 apiece?

Pomeroy: Yes.

Smokey: For 7 officers?

Pomeroy: Yes.

Smokey: 7 get 13?

Pomeroy: Uh-huh.

Smokey: You've only got 28.

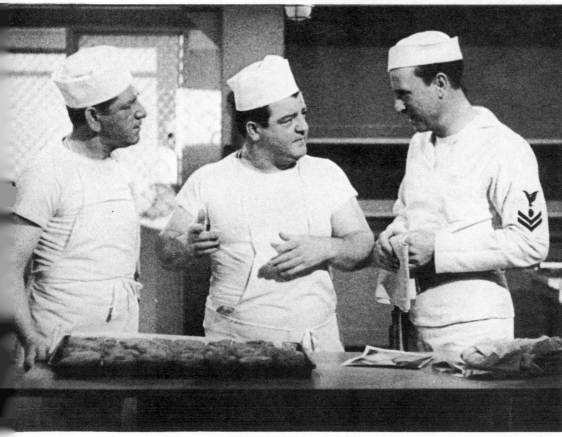

Pomeroy: That's right. I got 28 doughnuts and 7 — 13. I've got to give 'em to them.

Smokey: 7 thirteens are 28 — are they?

Pomeroy: Yes.

Smokey: That's ridiculous.

Pomeroy: It's got to be right.

Smokey: 7 times 4 is 28 — not 7 times 13.

Pomeroy: 7 times 4 is 28?

Smokey: Sure.

Pomeroy: 7 times 4 is 28. He must have went to a cheap school. I mean 7 times — 7 times 13 is 28.

Smokey: That's ridiculous.

Pomeroy: Come here. I'll figure it out for you.

Smokey: What's the matter with you?

Pomeroy: I've got this all figured out — look here.

Smokey: You have?

Pomeroy: Yeh, I figured it out myself. Look —

Smokey: Prove that to me.

Pomeroy: I'm going to prove it to you.

Pomeroy: Don't worry.

Smokey: Ridiculous.

Pomeroy: No, it ain't — no, it aint'.

Smokey: Oh — come — come.

Pomeroy: No, it ain't — it's not ridiculous.

Smokey: Theres' no sense to it.

Pomeroy: There is so.

Smokey: Go ahead.

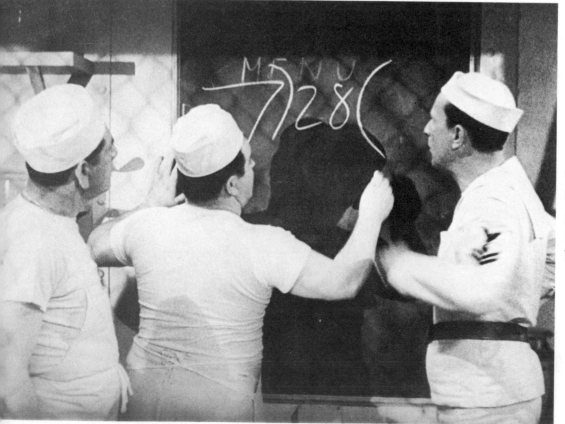

Pomeroy: You'll see. Now there are seven officers.

Smokey: That's right.

Pomeroy: There's the 7 — now I'm going to divide to prove it to you. 28 doughnuts —

Smokey: 28 doughnuts. Now wait a minute. You claim that 7 goes into 28 13 times?

Pomeroy: Uh-huh.

Smokey: Prove it to me.

Pomeroy: 7 into 2 — 7 will not go into 2 no matter how much you try.

Smokey: We know that.

Pomeroy: You can't push that big 7 into a little bit of a 2.

Smokey: Certainly not.

Pomeroy: Therefore we can't use the 2.

Pomeroy: I'm going to let Dizzy hold it. You hold that 2 for me, will you, please? Thank you. I'll use it later.

Smokey: What is this all about?

Pomeroy: Now 7 into 8 — 1.

Smokey: Once.

Pomeroy: Now we're going to carry the 7 —

Smokey: Carry the 7 —

Pomeroy: Carry the 7 —

Smokey: The 7 —

Pomeroy: It's got a little heavy so I'll put it right down and 7 from 8 —

Smokey: One.

Pomeroy: One. Now a minute ago — I couldn't use the 2.

Smokey: What do you mean?

Pomeroy: I'm going to use it now.

Smokey: Use it?

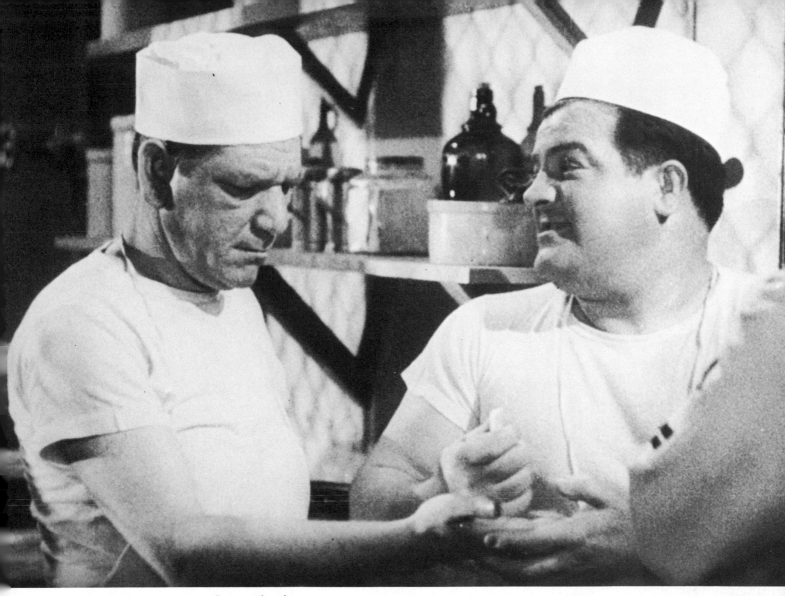

Pomeroy: Dizzy, give me that 2. Thanks.

Pomeroy: Right down there.

Smokey: Sooo?

Pomeroy: 7 into 21 —
Smokey: Three times.
Pomeroy: 3 times 7 — 28 — 13.

Smokey: Oh, now wait a minute. Come here — didn't you ever go to school, stupid?

Pomeroy: Yeh, and I come out the same way.

Smokey: Oh, never mind that.

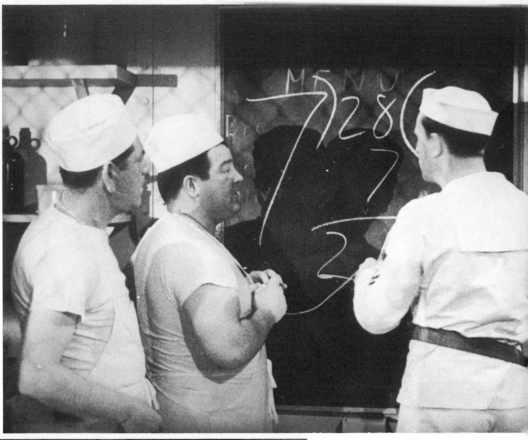

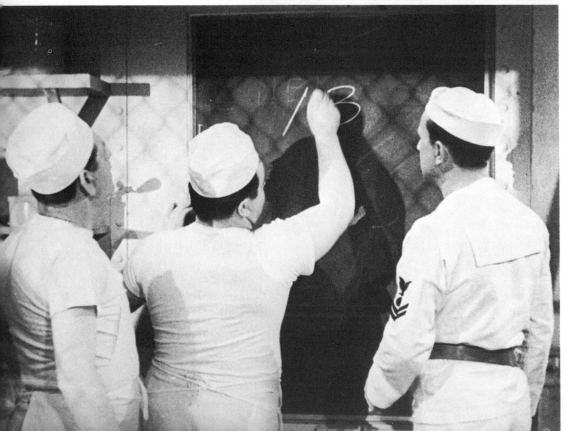

Smokey: Multiply this —

Pomeroy: Yes —

Smokey: Put down 13 officers.

Pomeroy: 13 it is.

Smokey: Now, you claim that each officer gets 13 doughnuts.

Pomeroy: He got it.

Smokey: Now wait a minute.

Pomeroy: Looks like we're going in the brig.

Smokey: And there are 7 officers — put down 7.

Pomeroy: 7.

Smokey: Draw a line.

Pomeroy: Sure.

Smokey: Now 7 times 13 is what?

Pomeroy: 28. 7 times 3 —

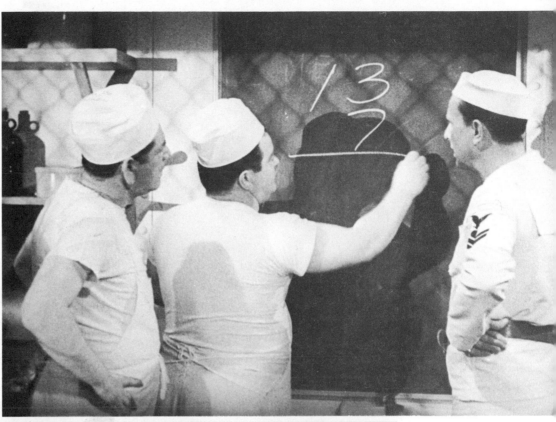

Smokey: 21.

Pomeroy: 7 times 1.

Smokey: 7.

Pomeroy: 7 and 1?

Smokey: 8.

Pomeroy: 28.

Smokey: Oh come on.

Pomeroy: It's all right. I knew it all the time.

Smokey: Well, it shouldn't come out right.

Pomeroy: It's got to come out right or I'll be going to the brig. That — I know.

Smokey: Just a minute. We'll add this up.

Smokey: Write 13 — 7
times —

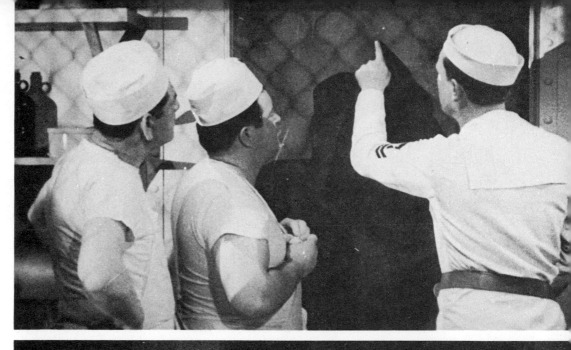

Pomeroy: Okay, that's
once — two.

Smokey: 2.

Pomeroy: 3 - 4 - 5 - 6 —

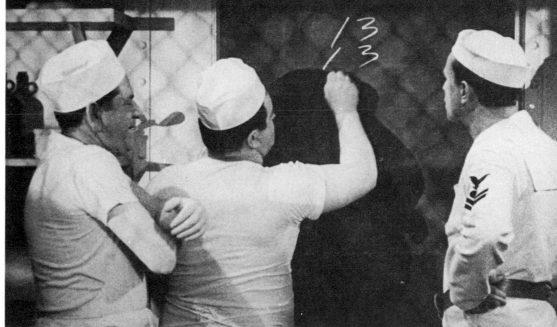

Smokey: Oh, oh, wait
a minute —

Pomeroy: Oh, I forgot —

Smokey: Yes?

Pomeroy: Dynamite — I
mustn't forget him.

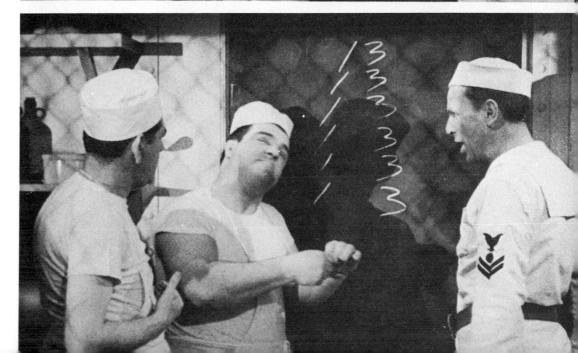

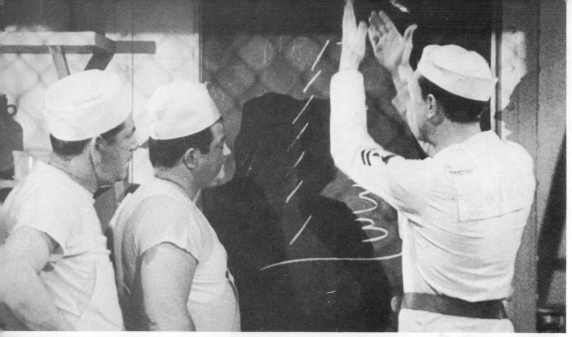

Smokey: No — there's 7 officers. Now, we're getting it. All this added up amounts to what?

Pomery: 28.

Smokey: Give me the chalk.

Pomeroy: No, if you take it, it's liable to come out right.

Smokey: Sure. Sure — there's something in that.

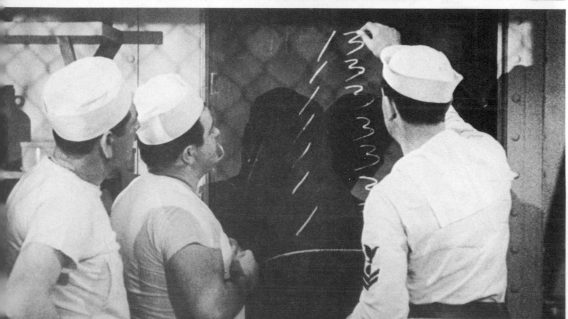

Smokey: 3-6-9-12-15-18-21 —

Pomeroy: 22-23-24-25-26-27-28 —

Smokey: Oh!

Pomeroy: See?

BUD ABBOTT
AND
LOU COSTELLO
in
"KEEP 'EM
FLYING"
COPYRIGHT MCMXLI BY UNIVERSAL PICTURES COMPANY, INC.

Blackie (Abbott) and Heathcliff (Costello) have only limited funds for lunch. Their plan goes wrong much, to the consternation of the waitress (Martha Raye).

Waitress: Won't you boys have something to eat?   **Heath:** Yes, ma'am, I want —

Blackie: Here. Please, please, what do you mean — yes, ma'am?

Blackie: We've only got a quarter, you know that? Don't you understand? What's wrong with you?

Heath: Well, a quarter — we can get something to eat.

Blackie: Well, I tell you what I'll do. I'll order a turkey sandwich and a cup of coffee, see? And I'll give you half. But, if she asks you if you want anything you say — no, I don't care for anything.

Heath: And if she asks me if I want something I say I don't care for nothing.

Blackie: Um-hum. that's right.

Heath: You mean we're going to put something over on her?

Blackie: No, no, we're not putting anything over on her.

Heath: Going to try to slick her?

Blackie: All we've got is a quarter.

Heath: She'll think we're a couple of big shots.

Blackie: That's the boy, come on.

Heath: I don't care for nothing.

Blackie: That's right.

Blackie: Give me a turkey sandwich and a cup of coffee, please.

Waitress: What will you have?

Heath: I don't care for nothing.

Blackie: Aw, go ahead, have something. **Heath:** Give me a turkey sandwich.

Blackie: What did I just get through telling you?

Heath: I refused once, didn't I? That's enough.

Blackie: I know, but we've only got a quarter.

Heath: I know but the waitress says to me — go ahead and have something. I said I don't care for nothing; and then —

Blackie: Never mind that. You can't order. Never mind what I say.

Heath: No matter how much you coax me?

Blackie: No matter how much I coax you. You just say I don't want anything.

Heath: I'll say I'm filled up, that's all.

Blackie: That's all. We've only got a quarter.

Heath: I ain't but I'll say I am.

Blackie: Well, say that.

Health: Okay.

Blackie: And I'll give you half my turkey sandwich.

Heath: I dont care for nothing.

Blackie: That turkey sandwich and a cup of coffee please.

Waitress: And what will you have?

Heath: I don't care for nothing.

Blackie: Oh, go ahead and have something.

Blackie: Go on, have something. Go on, Heathcliffe, you're in here to eat, right?

Heath: Yeah.

Blackie: Well, order something.　　**Heath:** Give me some ham and eggs.

Blackie: What did I just get through telling you?

Heath: What do you keep coaxing me for?

Blackie: Wait just a minute. We've only got a quarter.

Heath: I know but don't keep saying — go ahead take something. And I say I don't care for any —

Blackie: Never mind.

Heath: You say go ahead and have something.

Blackie: Never mind. Never mind what I say. Just don't order anything. How are you going to pay for it?

Heath: I'm filled up. I don't know from nothing.

Blackie: That's the idea. No matter how much I coax you, you don't want anything.

Heath: Then I'm deaf. I don't say nothing. Not a word.

Blackie: All right. Keep quiet. You order a sandwich! You can't pay for two turkey sandwiches, now can you?

Heath: I don't care for nothing.

Blackie: You don't want anything. That turkey sandwich and a cup of coffee, please.

Waitress: And what will you have?

Heath: I don't care for nothing.

Blackie: Oh sure you do.

Heath: Now stop asking me. I dont care for nothing. That's all. I'm not in the mood to eat.

Blackie: You told me you were hungry.

Heath: I know. I told you a lot of things but I ain't going to eat.

Blackie: Well, are you hungry?

Blackie: You are hungry. Now, look, you're in a restaurant, what do people go to restaurants for?

Heath: Not me, I'm just —

Blackie: What do people go to a restaurant for?

Heath: Sometimes I wonder.

Blackie: They go there to eat.

Heath: Yeah, eat.

Blackie: That's what you're here for.

Heath: That's a wonderful word — eat.

Blackie: All right, order something.

Heath: I'm not hungry.

Blackie: Now, listen do you want people to think I'm a cheap skate around here? Now go on and order something. Order something small.

Heath: Give me a small steak.

152

Blackie: What'd I just get through telling you?

Heath: Huh? What do you keep coaxing me for?

Blackie: Never mind that coaxing — no matter how much I coax you — you don't want anything.

Blackie: Now sit down there and behave yourself. A turkey sandwich and a cup of coffee, please.

Waitress: A turkey sandwich and a cup of coffee?

Blackie: Yes.

Waitress: Yes.

Blackie: He doesn't care
for anything.

Waitress: Yes.

Blackie: Thanks a lot.

Heathcliff finally gets the girl.

Gloria: Let's have a dance.　　　　**Heath:** I don't want to dance.　　**Gloria:** What's the matter?

Heath: I have a better idea. Do you mind — go out on the porch?

Gloria: What's the matter? Don't you like dancing?

Heath: No. It's just a whole lot of huggin' set to music.

Gloria: But what don't you like about that?

Heath: The music.

Gloria: Aw, Heathcliff!

Heath: Miss Phelps.

Gloria: Aw, please — you can call me anything you want.

Heath: I can call you anything I want? Okay, Gloria, you can call me anything you want.

Gloria: Okay, jerk come on!

a short take...

Heath: Blackie — I never took a drink in my life, but right now I feel like getting drunk.

Blackie: No!

Heath: I do, really.

Blackie: NO! You don't want a drink. Remember, every time you go into a bar room the devil goes in . . . with you.

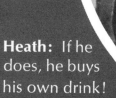

Heath: If he does, he buys his own drink!

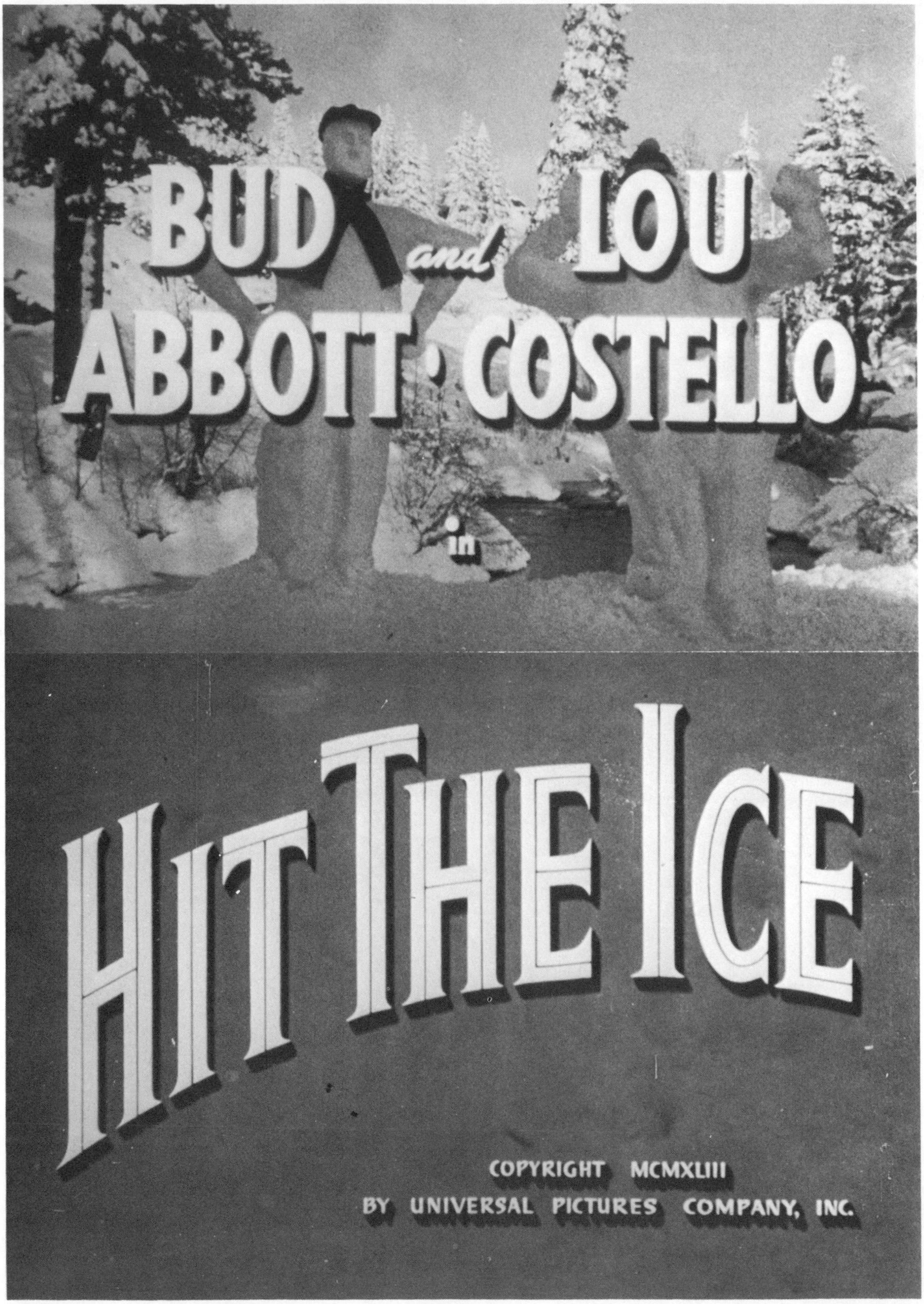
BUD and LOU
ABBOTT · COSTELLO
in
HIT THE ICE
COPYRIGHT MCMXLIII
BY UNIVERSAL PICTURES COMPANY, INC.

Having stumbled into a deserted bank, Flash (Abbott) and Tubby (Costello) try to find a teller.

Flash: Teller!

Flash: Teller!   **Tubby:** Tell who?   **Flash:** Teller!   **Tubby:** I'll tell 'er. Where is she?

Flash: Where is who? I said teller!

Tubby: Tell 'er what?

Flash: Tell 'er nothing. I want the teller.

Tubby: Well, go ahead and tell 'er — I don't care.

Flash: No! Teller in a bank!

Tubby: Tell 'er in a bank. Tell 'er outside. Tell 'er any place you want! I won't listen.

Flash: Listen — when I say "teller" I don't mean "tell 'er."

Tubby: Well, what do you mean?

Flash: Teller.

Tubby: Teller.

Flash: Now you've got it!

Tubby: Now I've got it! I don't even know what I'm talking about.

Flash proves that Tubby "couldn't whip cream with an outboard motor" in a typical Abbott and Costello bit.

Flash: You couldn't whip cream with an outboard motor.

Tubby: Is that so?

Flash: And I'll prove it to you. Here — do you see this handkerchief?

Tubby: What are ya got — a cold?

Flash: Never mind — a cold, I'll place it on the floor like that. I'll stand on one end of it — you stand on the other and I'll bet you can't hit me.

Tubby: You mean you're gonna put the handkerchief on the floor — you're gonna stand on one end and I'll stand on the other? — and I can't hit you?

Flash: That's right.

Tubby: With both of us standing on it?

Flash: That's right.

Tubby: What'll you bet?

Flash: Five dollars.

Tubby: Okay.

Flash: Put up your money. I'll hold it.

Tubby: Right.

Tubby: Watch what's back of you — cause I don't want to hurt you when I hit you.

Flash: Don't worry about that.

Tubby: Okay, kid.

Flash: Now look, kid. Don't you hit me till I say ready.

Tubby: I'll wait till you say it.

Flash: Now — no cheating.

Tubby: Oh — no — no.

Flash: Remember — no cheating.

Tubby: I'm standing on it right here.

Flash: Okay.

Tubby: I got my whole half a foot — I've got a whole half side here.

Tubby: Oh boy, I'll knock him cold.

Flash: Go ahead and hit me.

Flash: All right, I'm standing on the handkerchief.

Tubby: Whatta ya got the door here for?
What do you mean, shutting that door?

Later, Tubby tries to rework the bit to his favor.

Buster: I ought to take a poke at you.

Tubby: Why, you couldn't fight your way out of an outboard motor with whipped cream,— whipped cream?

Tubby: On second thought, I don't think you can do it.

Buster: Do what?

Tubby: Bop me in the nose.

Buster: Oh, can't I?

Tubby: No.

Buster: Just stand back.

Tubby: Wait — you wanna make a wager?

Buster: Sure, I'll make a wager.

Tubby: What's your share of that?

Buster: Ten G's.

Tubby: That's all I wanted to know — 10 G's — There's your 10 G's — put it on the table. Throw it on the table — don't count it. It's there. I know it.

Tubby: Here's mine. You got it?

Buster: Yes.

Tubby: Im going to get a handkerchief. Who's got one?

Fellowsby: Here's one.

Tubby: Thank you ever so much kid.

Tubby: See this handkerchief?

Buster: Yeah.

Tubby: I'm going to put it on the floor. You're gonna stand on one end — I'm gonna stand on the other and I'll bet you can't touch me.

Buster: You bet your cut against mine that if we two stand on the handkerchief I can't touch you?

Tubby: You got the idea.

Buster: Yeh.

Tubby: You're willing to bet?
Buster: You're gonna get a bet.
Tubby: That's all I wanted to know, brother.

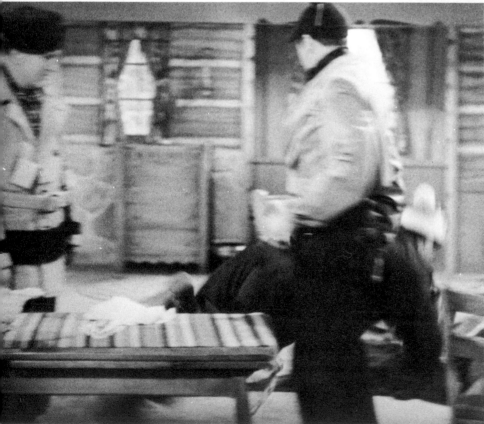

Tubby: Now listen, Shorty don't push — you're going to get your chance.

Tubby: Now listen to me, wise guy. I'll tell you, here I'll put the handkerchief on the floor.

Tubby: Now you stand on that edge right over there — stand on the edge of the handkerchief — that's it.

Tubby: I'll put my two feet here.

Tubby: Now listen — are you ready? When you're ready — you try and catch me.

Tubby: Oh, wait a minute
— wait a minute.

Tubby: I forgot something
— wait a minute.

Tubby: Not here — not here — come on.

Tubby: You stand over there — right over there. I come pretty near getting killed.

Tubby: I got it all fixed. Now then you stand on the edge of the handkerchief right here.

Tubby: Ready!

Tubby: When I say ready — you try and touch me.

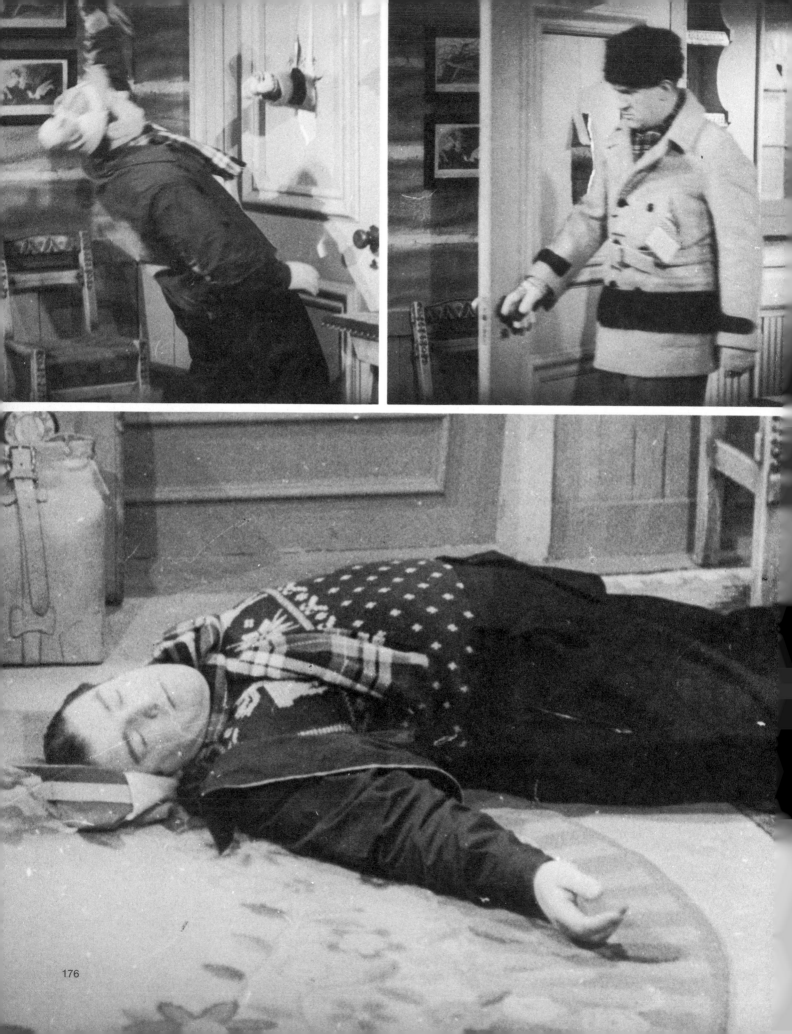

Grover: What're you doing? What's wrong with you? Do you know you were driving over thirty-five miles an hour?

Wilbur: A minute!

Grover: Thiry-five miles an hour!

Wilbur: A minute! This car won't go an hour!

Grover (Abbott) gives Wilbur (Costello) a lesson about a horse.

Princess: Wilbur. You shouldn't give him peppermint candy to eat. It's bad for his teeth.

Wilbur: He likes peppermint candy.

Grover: Now, she's right. You'll spoil the horse's appetite. Now he won't eat his fodder.

Wilbur: Eat his fodder?

Grover: Uh-huh.

Wilbur: What do you think Finnegan is — a cannibal?

Grover: No — she's going to hang his fodder on his nose.

Wilbur: Ain't he going to look funny with his fodder on his nose?

Grover: He eats his fodder every day.

Wilbur: Finnegan eats his fodder every day.

Grover: Well — sure.

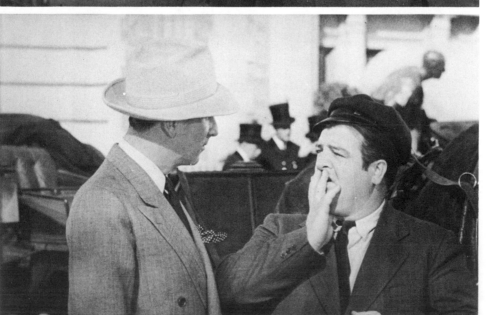

Wilbur: And what does his fodder eat?

Grover: He eats his fodder.

Wilbur: Oh — and what's his mother eat?

Grover: Why she eats her fodder.

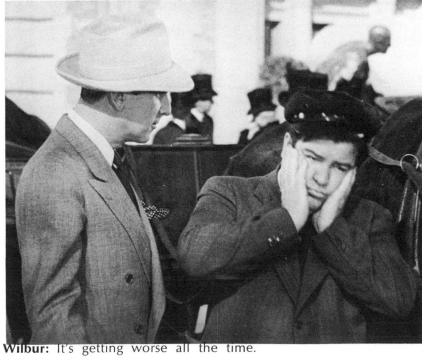

Wilbur: It's getting worse all the time.

Grover: Oh, what's the use of talking to you?

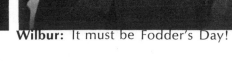

Wilbur: It must be Fodder's Day!

Finnegan is ill and Grover decides to play doctor.

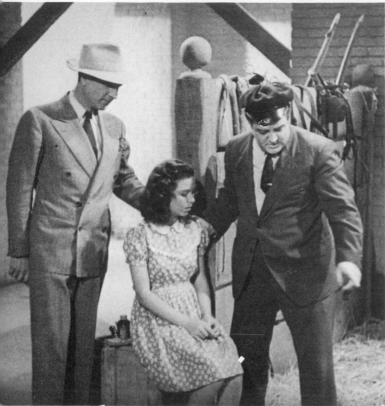

Wilbur: Come on. Sit down over here, dear. You've got nuthin' to worry about, honey. I'm gonna have Finnegan up and well in no time.

Grover: Sure he will. Well, get to work, horse doctor.

Grover: What are you doing?
Wilbur: Takin' his pulse.

Grover: Not there. In the front.

Wilbur: Oh, by his two front legs.

Grover: No, they're the horse's forelegs.

Wilbur: Forelegs? I said by his two front legs.

Grover: Well, the horse's forelegs are in front.

Wilbur: What's those things in the back, crutches?

Trying to buy a horse can get confusing.

Wilbur: Excuse me — I'm awfully sorry — but does it say in those papers there where you can get a good carriage horse?

Umbrella: Naw — these dope sheets just give you the horse's records.

Umbrella: — like if a horse has an X in front of his name that shows he's a mudder.

Wilbur: How can a he be a mudder? Ain't a she always a mudder?

Grover: No. Sometimes a he is a better mudder than a she.

Wilbur: A he makes a better mudder than a she? How can you tell if a horse is a mudder?

Grover: By looking at its feet.

Wilbur: Ain't we livin' in a wonderful age? Whoo! Mudder — Fodder —?

BUD ABBOTT
AND
LOU COSTELLO

IN SOCIETY
COPYRIGHT MCMXLIV BY UNIVERSAL PICTURES COMPANY, INC.

A classic vaudeville routine performed by Abbott (Ed) and Costello (Albert).

Ed: We've got to deliver these to the Susquehanna Hat Company.
Albert: Where is it?
Ed: It's on Beagle Street.
Albert: Where's Beagle Street?
Ed: I don't know. We'll ask somebody. It's on our way down.
Albert: How much did you say they were?
Ed: Seven-fifty apiece.
Albert: How do I look with a seven dollar and a half hat on?

Ed: Let me see. Kind of spiffy.
Albert: Okay.
Ed: All right. Carry those, but don't get them dirty.
Albert: Let's go.
Ed: Be careful.
Albert: Beagle Street, huh?
Ed: Beagle Street. We'll ask somebody.
Albert: We'll ask somebody.

187

Ed: Here — ask this fellow where Beagle street is.
Al: Okay. Excuse me — can you tell me where Beagle Street is?
Man: Sorry, buddy, I haven't got a dime.

Al: Who's asking you for money? I'm only asking you where Beagle Street is.

Man: Do I know where Beagle Street is? Of course I know where Beagle Street is. Do I look like I just got off a boat? Is there a tag on my lapel saying I just came from Ellis Island? Of course I know where Beagle Street is — I was born and raised on Beagle Street. My brother was born on Beagle Street. Do you know my brother?

Man: What right have you got to go around talking about my brother? I'll have you understand my brother is one of the finest boys that ever walked in shoe leather. My brother was an honor student in school.

Man: Go ahead. Say something nasty about my brother. Say something like he shouldn't get a parole.

Al: I'm asking you where Beagle Street is. That's — a — a common ordinary citizen just asks another fellow where Beagle Street is. I gotta deliver these hats to the Susquehanna Hat Company.

Man: Susquehanna Hat Company!
Al: Leave go of me. OHHH!

Man: Is that a Susquehanna Hat?
Al: Yeah.

Man: You know who makes these hats?
Al: I don'no — it —
Man: Child labor. Little girls — thirteen, fourteen years' old. Little girls with curls down to here. They work thirteen — fourteen hours a day. They work in a sweat shop all day long.

Man: Here's what I think of a Susquehanna hat.

Man: An look at it — look — look at that band.

Man: Imitation leather. Just like paper. And look.
Al: I wouldn't give you seven and a half dollars —
Man: Ow! Mmmm!
Al: What'sa matter?

Man: You stuck a wire in there for me to cut my finger. That's the worst thing I ever saw. Tell your Susquehanna Hat Company that's what I think of it!

Ed: Well, you know what that's going to cost you,
Al: Give 'em back to Dan.
Ed: Seven dollars and fifty cents.

Ed: You broke one of Dan's hats.
Al: Look! All I did was put a hat on my head. Did I ask the guy to take it off?

Ed: That's enough. It's the way you ask them.
Al: You ask the next guy.
Ed: Come on — never mind. Let's find Beagle Street.

Ed: Here. Ask this lady where Beagle Street is.

Al: 'scuse me, lady. Could you tell me where Beagle Street is?

Lady: Beagle Street. Oh, why did you have to remind me of Beagle Street?

Lady: My husband was killed on Beagle Street. Do you hear? My husband was killed on Beagle Street.

Al: I mean — but what — what — I don't know what I mean. I don't — I don't understand this at all. All I doo — I wanta — I wanta go to the — the — the Susquehanna Hat Company.

Lady: The Susquehanna Hat Company!

Lady: Is that a Susquehanna Hat?

Lady: That was the same kind of hat my husband was wearing when he was killed. And he wouldn't have lost his life if he had been wearing a good hat, when the safe fell out of that fifteen story building.

Lady: But no! He was wearing a hat like this one.

Lady: Oh! That's the cheapest — the worst grade of straw — I ever saw!

Lady: Oh, my husband's dead. He's dead! He's dead!

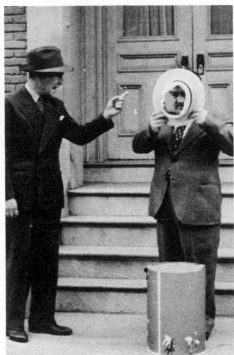

Al: He ain't dead, lady; he's hiding.
Ed: Now, listen.
Al: That guy —

Ed: Just a minute. That's two hats you've broken. Now, do you know how much you owe Derby Dan?

Al: No. How much do I owe Derby Dan, now?
Ed: Fifteen dollars.
Al: Fifteen dollars?
Ed: Yeah. And stop insulting women.

Al: Look. All I asked her is where was Beagle Street.
Ed: Yeah.

Woman: Beagle Street. Don't ever mention that name.

Woman: I can't — Beagle Street!

Ed: Wait a minute. Will you hold that still?

Al: Take back the hats.

Ed: Take that — take that box — Now go on down there and find out where Beagle Street is.

Al: Hey, Eddy!
Ed: What?
Al: How much do I owe Dan now?
Ed: Twenty-two dollars and fifty cents.
Al: I'm going to try just one more.
Ed: Better not. But be careful with that one. Will you, please?

Ed: Hey, wait a minute. I've got an idea. I'm going to run back to our plumbing shop and get some of those little business cards of ours. And we'll give them away to those Society people up at Briarwood.
Al: Very good business idea that you've got, Eddy.
Eddy: Yes, but find out where Beagle Street is, please.
Al: Okay. I'll ask another guy that comes along. I'll ask anybody. I don't care.

Al: Excuse me, Mister. Could you please tell me where Beagle Street is?

Man: Beagle Street?
Don't ask me where
Beagle Street is. A terrible
thing happened to me
on Beagle Street.

Man: I was walking along
minding my own business
and a safe fell from a
fifteen-story building on
my head — and killed me!

Al: A safe fell fifteen
floors and fell on your
head and killed you?
Man: Yes.
Al: Then, as long as
you're dead, there's no
use asking you where the
Susquehanna Hat
Company is.

Man: Susquehanna Hat Company!!! That's the hat I was wearing the day that I was killed.

Man: You're asking me about the — I'm so sorry. — I think . . . I've broken your hat.

Man: And you ask me about — That's the one I was wearing — that's the kind of a hat I was wearing —

Al: You think you've broken it?
Man: Yes.
Al: This is the Fourth Susquehanna Hat I —   **Man:** Susquehanna Hat Company!

Al: Oh!

Luigi: Get out of here! What are you trying to do to my shop? You trying to ruin my place? Police!!! Help! Help! Police!

Man: Why you —

Policeman: Hey, what's going on here?

Luigi: This fellow here — that big fellow — he hit the little fellow, my friend.

Policeman: Come on, you. Oh, a tough guy, huh?
Man: Wait a minute. Wait a minute.

Policeman: You're going with me.
Man: You can't take me to jail.
Policeman: Oh, no?
Man: You can't take me to jail. I'm dead. Ha, ha! You can't take me to jail.
Policeman: Come on, boy.

Luigi: He's crazy.
Al: Yes, he's crazy.

Luigi: Yeah, now, what can I do for you, Albert?
Al: Luigi, how can I get to the Susquehanna Hat Company?

Luigi: Susquehanna!

Al: Luigi! Oh, Luigi!

Luigi: Susquehanna! Susquehanna!

Having been inadvertently invited to a society ball, the boys are shown to their room by the butler (Arthur Treacher — who else?).

Pipps: Here's your room, Gentlemen. I hope you like it.
Eddy: Quite.

Al: Who ever wouldn't like this room? You mean this one room for the two of us? And another thing —

Eddy: What's the matter?
Al: Who cut this bed in half?

Eddy: Oh, they're twin beds.
Al: Do we look like twins?
Eddy: Now, keep quiet.

Pipps: Of course, we have a very rigorous schedule here. You bathe at ten; you brunch at eleven; you tea at two —

Al: You must have a very very ridgorous shed gool. I always do. I wash basin at eight; and then I doughnut at nine; I pinball machine at ten; I hamburger and onions at eleven; and I bicarbonate of soda at twelve.

Pipps: That settles everything.   **Al:** It sure does.

Eddy: Pay no attention to my friend here. He's very "essentric". He's very very wealthy.

Pipps: If you'll pardon me, gentlemen. I'll be back in a moment.

Eddy: Yes, sure.

Al: Say!
Eddy: What's the matter?
Al: The Winthrops. They're very fine people.
Eddy: Yes.
Al: Look at all the nice clothes they're lending us.
Eddy: Well, let them think we're used to it. Don't act surprised.

Eddy: And remember your etiquette.
Al: Etiquette?

Eddy: Etiquette.
Al: You're trying to tell me? You can't learn me nothing like that.

Al: You don't even know how to say the word. Not etiquette . . .

Eddy: Etiquette?
Al: No . . . ah-tick-it-tee.
Eddy: No! Etiquette!
Al: Ah-tick-it-tee.
Eddy: I said "Etiquette"!
Al: You don't have to tell me about all that stuff because my Mother told me the right road from the wrong road. And if my Mother thought I was going to be wrong, she always told me. Because I had the right kind of bringing up.

Pipps: Gentlemen, your bath is drawn.
Al: Erase it.

Pipps: Er-what?
Al: Rub it out.

Eddy: Shhh! Not so loud. My friend is very humorous, too. You've got to take a bath.
Al: Quiet. Not so loud.

Some good deeds can be quite unrewarding.

Drunk: Save me! Help! Help! Help!

213

Al: Follow me, boy!

Al: Go ahead, kid. Go on.   **Al:** Get up!

Drunk: I'm going to sue you in every court in this world!
Al: What's the matter? Didn't I just save your life?

Drunk: Yeah — but where's my hat?

Ed: What in the world is this?
Al: How do you like this guy? I just saved his life!
Ed: You saved who's life?
Al: His!

Ed: Do you know this
guy?
Al: No.

Ed: You had no business
— going out there! You
had no license to go out
after that man!

Al: Whatta ya mean? You
gotta have a license to
go save a guy?
Ed: Listen — his —
Al: I mean — after all —
whatta ya want me to do
— run down town to the
bureau and say, 'Gimme
a license — I want to jump
in and save a man'?

Ed: Don't you know there's lifeguards. They've got families. Those families depend on the salaries that those life guards earn. They jump in swimming pools and oceans and save people. And you — as soon as their back is turned — you deliberately sneak into the pool and do the work for nothing! Don't ever do a thing like that. Don't ever —

Al: I — I'm sorry I saved you.
Ed: You should be sorry.
Drunk: Pardon me, gentlemen. Pardon me.
Would you mind —

Drunk: Would you mind very much if I
settled this argument?
Al: I wish you would. You tell Eddy everything.
Go ahead.
Drunk: Thank you very much.

Ed: Now, that's better.

BUD ABBOTT

LOU COSTELLO

in

"THE NAUGHTY NINETIES"

Copyright MCMXLV By Universal Pictures Company, Inc.

Bud Abbott (Dexter Broadhurst) and Lou Costello (Sebastian Dinwiddie) perform their classic "Who's on First?" routine.

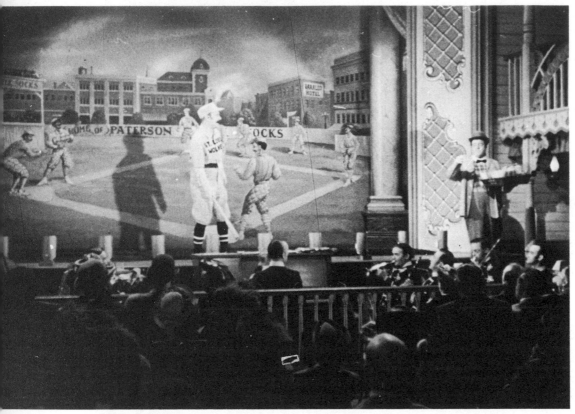

Sebastian: Peanuts!
Dexter: Peanuts!
Sebastian Popcorn!
Dexter: Popcorn!
Sebastian: Crackerjack!
Dexter: Crackerjack!
Sebastian: Get your packages of crackerjack here!
Dexter: — crackerjack — will you keep quiet? Sebastian! Sebastian, please! Don't interrupt my act!
Dexter: Sebastian!

Sebastian: Oh, Mr. Broadhurst, I didn't see the lights there. I forgot about 'em.
Dexter: What in the world are you doing? Why interrupt my act like this?

Sebastian: Look, Mr. Broadhurst, I mean after all — if you're in a ball park — they always sell peanuts and popcorns and things like that.

Dexter: I know that, Sebastian, but not in front of — I — beg — I beg your pardon please.

Sebastian: Ladies and gentlemen and also the children — will you excuse me for a minute, please? Thank you.

Dexter: What do you want to do?
Sebastian: Look, Mr. Broadhurst —
Dexter: What are you doing?
Sebastian: I love baseball!
Dexter: Well, we all love baseball.

Sebastian: When we get to St. Louis, will you tell me the guys' names on the team so when I go to see them in that St. Louis ball park I'll be able to know those fellows?

Dexter: Well, now—is it all right, folks? All right.
Sebastian: Excuse me.
Dexter: All right.

Sebastian: I wanta — I wanta find out the fellows' names

Dexter: As long as it's okay with the audience.

Sebastian: I'm crazy about baseball.

Dexter: Will you stand still? Pick up your hat!
Go pick up your hat.

Sebastian: Okay.

Dexter: Now look. Then you'll go
and peddle your popcorn and don't
interrupt the act any more?

Sebastian: Yes sir.

223

Dexter: Now, on the St. Louis team we have Who's on first, What's on second, I Don't Know is on third —

Sebastian: That's what I want to find out. I want you to tell me the names of the fellows on the St. Louis team.

Dexter: I'm telling you. Who's on first, What's on second, I Don't Know is on third —

Dexter: All right. But you know, strange as it may seem, they give ball players nowadays very peculiar names.

Sebastian: Funny names?

Dexter: Nicknames. Nicknames.

Sebastian: Not — not as funny as my name — Sebastian Dinwiddie.

Dexter: Oh, yes, yes, yes!

Sebastian: Funnier than that?

Dexter: Oh, absolutely. Yes.

Sebastian: You know the fellows' names?
Dexter: Yes.

Sebastian: Well, then, who's playin' first?
Dexter: Yes.
Sebastian: I mean the fellow's name on first base.
Dexter: Who.

Sebastian: The fellow playin' first base for St. Louis.
Dexter: Who.
Sebastian: The guy on first base.

Dexter: Who is on first.
Sebastian: Well, what are you askin' me for?

Dexter: I'm not asking you — I'm telling you. **Who is on first.**
Sebastian: I'm asking you — who's on first?

Dexter: That's the man's name!
Sebastian: That's who's name?
Dexter: Yes.
Sebastian: Well, go ahead and tell me!

Dexter: Who.
Sebastian: The guy on first.
Dexter: Who.
Sebastian: The first baseman.
Dexter: Who is on first.

Sebastian: Have you got a first baseman on first?
Dexter: Certainly.
Sebastian: Then who's playing first?
Dexter: Absolutely.

Sebastian: When you pay off the first baseman every month, who gets the money?
Dexter: Every dollar of it. And why not, the man's entitled to it.

Sebastian: Who is?
Dexter: Yes.
Sebastian: So who gets it?
Dexter: Why shouldn't he? Sometimes his wife comes down and collects it.
Sebastian: Who's wife?
Dexter: Yes.

Dexter: After all the man earns it.
Sebastian: Who does?
Dexter: Absolutely.

Sebastian: Well all I'm trying to find out is what's the guy's name on first base.

Dexter: Oh, no, no, What is on Second Base.

Sebastian: I'm not asking you who's on second.
Dexter: Who's on first.
Sebastian: That's what I'm trying to find out.
Dexter: Well, don't change the players around.

Sebastian: I'm not changing nobody.
Dexter: Now, take it easy.
Sebastian: What's the guy's name on first base?

Dexter: What's the guy's name on second base.
Sebastian: I'm not askin' ya who's on second.
Dexter: Who's on first.
Sebastian: I don't know.
Dexter: He's on third. We're not talking about him.

Sebastian: How could I get on third base?

Dexter: You mentioned his name.

Sebastian: If I mentioned the third baseman's name, who did I say is playing third?

Dexter: No, Who's playing first.

Sebastian: Stay offa first will ya?

Dexter: Well what do you want me to do?

Sebastian: Now what's the guy's name on first base?

Dexter: What's on second.

Sebastian: I'm not asking ya who's on second.

Dexter: Who's on first.

Sebastian: I don't know.

Dexter: He's on third.

Sebastian: There I go back on third again.

Dexter: Well, I can't change their names.

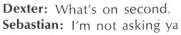

231

Sebastian: Say, will you please stay on third base Mr. Broadhurst.
Dexter: Please. Now what is it you want to know?
Sebastian: What is the fellow's name on third base?
Dexter: What is the fellow's name on second base.
Sebastian: I'm not askin' ya who's on second.

Dexter: Who's on first.
Sebastian: I dont' know.
Dexter and Sebastian: Third Base!

Sebastian: You got an outfield?
Dexter: Oh, sure.
Sebastian: St. Louis has got a good outfield?
Dexter: Oh, absolutely.
Sebastian: The left fielder's name?
Dexter: Why.

Sebastian: I don't know, I just thought I'd ask.
Dexter: Well, I just thought I'd tell you.
Sebastian: Then tell me who's playing left field.
Dexter: Who's playing first.
Sebastian: Stay out of the infield.
Dexter: Don't mention any names out here.
Sebastian: I want to know what's the fellow's name on left field.
Dexter: What is on second.
Sebastian: I'm not asking you who's on second.
Dexter: Who is on first.
Sebastian: I don't know.

Dexter and Sebastian: Third Base!

Dexter: Now take it easy, take it easy man.
Sebastian: And the left fielder's name?
Dexter: Why.
Sebastian: Because.
Dexter: Oh, he's Center Field.

Dexter: He's Center. Will you pick up your hat please.
Sebastian: Center Field.
Dexter: Pick up your hat. And stop this —
Now look, please.

Sebastian: Mr. Broadhurst.
Dexter: Yes?
Sebastian: Wait a minute. You got a pitcher on the team?
Dexter: Wouldn't this be a fine team without a pitcher.
Sebastian: I don't know. Tell me the pitcher's name.

Dexter: I'm telling you man.
Sebastian: Then go ahead.
Dexter: Tomorrow.
Sebastian: What time?

Dexter: What time what?
Sebastian: What time tomorrow are you gonna tell me who's pitching?

Dexter: Now listen, Who is not pitching. Who is on —

Dexter: Tomorrow.
Sebastian: You don't want to tell me today?

Dexter: What's on second.
Sebastian: I don't know.

Sebastian and Dexter: Third Base!

Sebastian: I'll break your arm if you say who's on first.
Dexter: Then why come up here and ask?
Sebastian: I want to know what's the pitcher's **name**.

Sebastian: You gotta Catcher?
Dexter: Yes.
Sebastian: The Catcher's name?
Dexter: Today.
Sebastian: Today. And Tommorow's pitching.
Dexter: Now you've got it.

Sebastian: That's all. St. Louis got a couple of days on their team. That's all.
Dexter: Well I can't help that. Alright. What do you want me to do?

Sebastian: Gotta catcher?
Dexter: Yes.
Sebastian: I'm a good catcher too you know.
Dexter: I know that.

Sebastian: I would like to play for the St. Louis team.
Dexter: Well I might arrange that.

Sebastian: I would like to catch. Now I'm being a good Catcher, tomorrow's pitching on the team, and I'm catching.
Dexter: Yes.

Sebastian: Tomorrow throws the ball and the guy up bunts the ball.
Dexter: Yes.
Sebastian: Now when he bunts the ball — me being a good catcher — I want to throw the guy out at first base, so I pick up the ball and throw it to who.

Dexter: Now, that's the first thing you've said right.

Sebastian: I DON'T EVEN KNOW WHAT I'M TALKING ABOUT.

Dexter: Well, that's all you have to do.
Sebastian: Is to throw it to first base.

Dexter: Yes.
Sebastian: Now who's got it?
Dexter: Naturally.

Sebastian: Who has it?
Dexter: Naturally.
Sebastian: Naturally.

Dexter: Naturally.
Sebastian: O.K.
Dexter: Now you've got it.

Sebastian: I pick up the ball and I throw it to Naturally.
Dexter: No you don't, you throw the ball to first base.
Sebastian: Then who gets it?
Dexter: Naturally.
Sebastian: O.K.
Dexter: Alright.
Sebastian: I throw the ball to Naturally.
Dexter: You don't. You throw it to Who.
Sebastian: Naturally.
Dexter: Well, naturally. Say it that way.
Sebastian: That's what I said.

Dexter: You did not.
Sebastian: I said I'd throw the ball to Naturally.
Dexter: You don't. You throw it to Who.
Sebastian: Naturally.
Dexter: Yes.
Sebastian: So I throw the ball to first base and Naturally gets it.
Dexter: No. You throw the ball to first base—
Sebastian: Then who gets it?
Dexter: Naturally.
Sebastian: That's what I'm saying.
Dexter: You're not saying that.
Sebastian: Excuse me folks.
Dexter: It's alright. I'm sorry folks.

Sebastian: I throw the ball to Naturally.
Dexter: You throw it to Who.
Sebastian: Naturally.
Dexter: Naturally. Well say it that way.
Sebastian: That's what I'm saying.

Dexter: Now don't get excited. Now don't get excited.
Sebastian: I throw the ball to first base.

Dexter: Then Who gets it.
Sebastian: He better get it.
Dexter: That's it. Alright now don't get exctied. Take it easy.
Sebastian: Hmmph.
Dexter: Hmmph.

Sebastian: Now I throw the ball to first base, who-ever it is grabs the ball, so the guy runs to second.
Dexter: Uh-huh.
Sebastian: Who picks up the ball and throws it to what. What throws it to I don't know. I don't know throws it back to tomorrow — a triple play.

Dexter: Yeah. It could be.
Sebastian: Another guy gets up and it's a long fly ball to center.

Sebastian: Why?

Sebastian: I don't know.

Sebastian: And I don't care.

Dexter: Oh, that's our shortstop!

Dexter: What was that?

Sebastian: I said, **I don't care.**

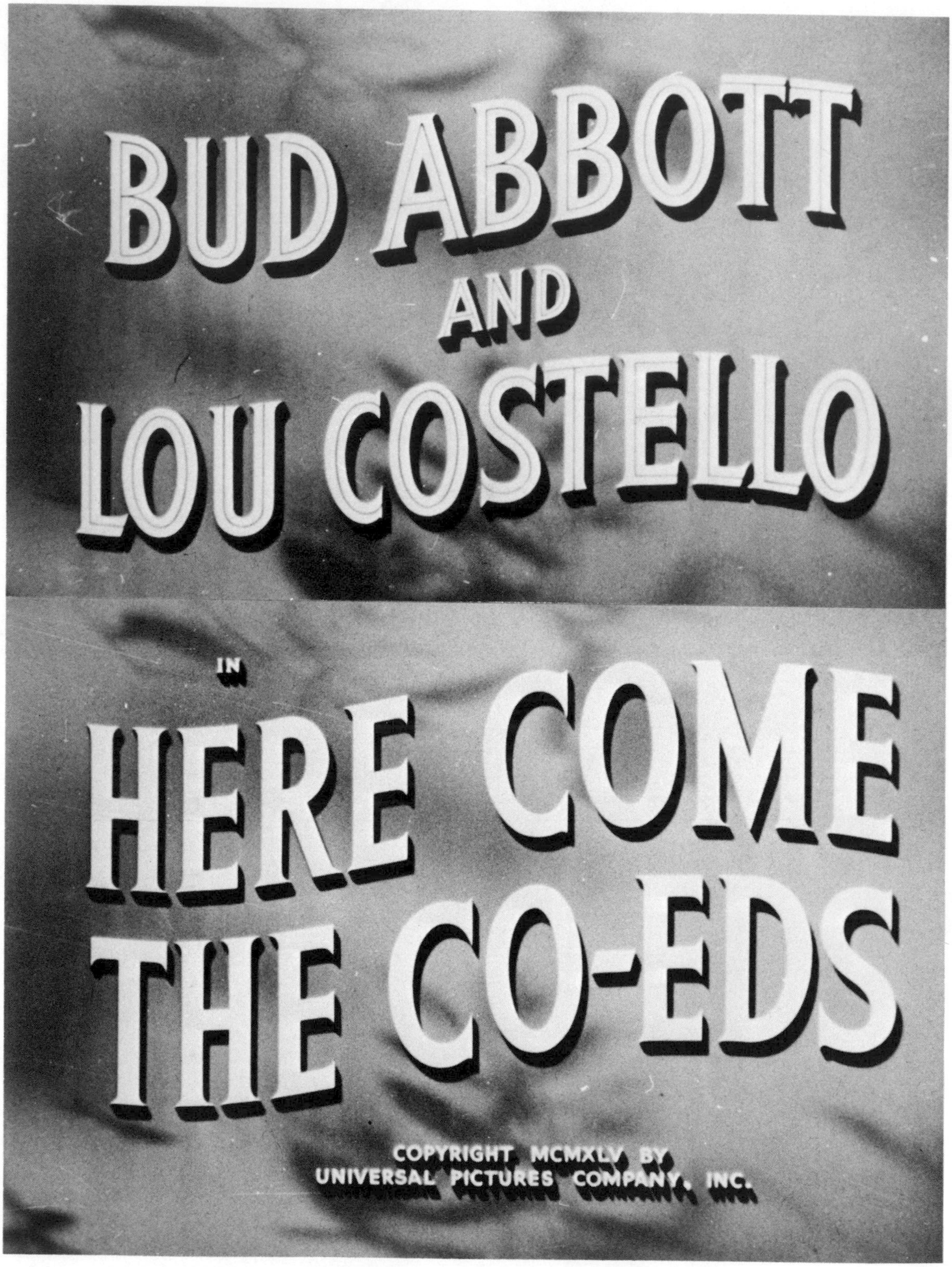
BUD ABBOTT
AND
LOU COSTELLO
IN
HERE COME
THE CO-EDS
COPYRIGHT MCMXLV BY
UNIVERSAL PICTURES COMPANY, INC.

Oliver (Costello) tries to tell a story. Slats (Abbott) gives him a hard time, as usual.

Oliver: I gotta joke.
Slats: You've got a joke?

Oliver: A brand new one I wrote myself.
Slats: Where did you get it?
Oliver: I wrote it.
Slats: Aw, stop.
Oliver: Yes, I did, Slats. I did.
Slats: You wrote a joke?
Oliver: It's a brand new joke, and I'd like to tell it to the girls for the first time. I think they'll like it.

Slats: Is it brand new?
Oliver: Maybe they can use it for the show.
Slats: Hey, that's a good idea.
Oliver: Yes, it is. I tell this one by myself. I — I don't need you.
Slats: Oh, that's all right. That's all right. But you say it's brand new?
Oliver: Yes.
Slats: Nobody's ever heard it?

Oliver: No. And I tell the story while you keep your mouth — shut. It's about a whale, a ship, and Jonah.
Slats: And it's brand new.
Oliver: Very brand new story. Yeah.
Stats: Um — huh.

Oliver: Now, once upon a time, there was a whale.

Slats: What kind of a whale?

Oliver: And this whale was — —

Slats: What kind of a whale?

Oliver: Hmm, a plain everyday whale.

Slats: It was? All right, I'm sorry.

Oliver: How do I know what kind a whale? What do you think I do, go around with whales or somethin'?

Slats: All right, all right. Shhh, please.

Oliver: Don't try to make a fool of me in front of the girls.

Slats: All right, go ahead.

Oliver: I mean a plain, everyday whale, that's all.

Slats: All right, so it was a whale.

Oliver: How do I know what kind of a whale?

Slats: All right!

Oliver: Now the whale was in the ocean —

Slats: What ocean?

Oliver: He was —

Slats: Well, wait a minute, I mean —

Oliver: Go on, pick out an ocean. Go ahead. **Slats:** That's immaterial to me. **Oliver:** All right, the Immaterial ocean. **Slats:** Aw, come on.

Oliver: Now, the whale was in the Immaterial ocean. He was minding his own business —— but he was followin' a ship.

Slats: What ship? **Oliver:** And this ship is — **Slats:** What ship?

Oliver: A ship that swims in the water.

Slats: You mean a swim ship?
Oliver: Yeah. Ohhh.

Oliver: Now the whale was followin' the swim ship because he — who ever heard of a swim ship?

Slats: I only — —

Oliver: I asked you to keep your mouth shut, didn't I?

Slats: You're telling the story.

Oliver: You're gettin' me mad!

Slats: Shhh, wait a minute. When do we laugh at this thing?

Oliver: They're laughin' before they're supposed to.

Oliver: Dont laugh now.
Slats: Ladies.
Oliver: I didn't say nothin' yet.
Slats: Ladies, be quiet. Go ahead, go ahead. Go ahead, let's hear it.
Oliver: Now, the whale was in the ocean. He was very hungry — — and Captain Jonah was the captain of the boat — —

Oliver: — and he didn't want the whale to capsize the boat.
Slats: What?
Oliver: To capsize the boat.
Slats: Capsize?
Oliver: — because — yeah, he — he didn't —
Slats: You know what that means?
Oliver: Sure. I don't — I don't put words like that in stories if I don't know what they are.
Oliver: He didn't want the whale to capsize the boat.
Slats: What does it mean? What — what does it mean?
Oliver: Capsize?
Slats: Capsize.
Oliver: That — that's a big word.
Slats: Well, what does it mean?

Slats: You know what it means?
Oliver: Oh, sure. That's a —
Slats: Well, what does it mean? What does capsize mean?
Oliver: It's a nice word.

Slats: Well, what does it mean?
Oliver: Capsize.
Slats: Capsize.
Oliver: That's like six and seven-eighth's — seven and a quarter —
Slats: All right, go ahead.

Oliver: — so he didn't want the whale to six and seven-eighth's the boat —
Slats: All right, all right, go ahead.
Oliver: See?

Oliver: So Captain Jonah is a captain of a boat, and he was afraid he was gonna lose some passengers — so then Captain Jonah figured the only thing he could do was throw over a barrel of apples.

Slats: What kind of apples?
Oliver: And — and —
Slats: What kind of — what kind of apples?
Oliver: Apples that grow on a tree.
Slats: Well, there's all kinds of apples. There's Baldwin apples — there's —
Oliver: Crabapples —
Slats: Well, tell the girls that.
Oliver: So he threw 'em over a barrel of crabapples.
Slats: Take it easy, take it easy.
Oliver: He's got me mad at you kids now.
Slats: Well, just let it go.

Oliver: So, after the whale ate the apples — the whale was still hungry — and then Captain Jonah figured the only thing he could do was throw the whale over the stool. What kind of a stool?

Slats: Who said that?
Oliver: I did. That's in case you asked me.

Oliver: He threw him over a three-legged camp stool. Now, the whale ate the apples — and the whale ate the stool —and the whale was still hungry. His appetite had not been appeased. Don't ask me what that is. I don't know.

Slats: I won't ask you. All right, go ahead.

Oliver: So after the whale ate the apples and the stool — and he ate the stool — the whale was still hungry — and the Captain Jonah figured the only way he could save his passengers and his boat, was to sacrifice himself.

Slats: Yes?

Oliver: And he did. He threw a beautiful jacknife dive right into the mouth of the whale. Now, the whale ate Captain Jonah — he ate the apples — and he ate the stool —

Slats: Ah, —

Oliver: — and then the whale swam away.

Oliver: Three years later they caught that very same whale —
Slats: Listen, Oliver, —
Oliver: — they cut him open —
Slats: Hey, wait a minute —
Oliver: — and what do you think they found —
Slats: Oliver — just wait a moment —
Oliver: — not now—not now — all right — he says something then I tell you the funny joke.

Slats: Wait a minute, Oliver, just a minute. Now you're not coming up here this afternoon, in front of these girls, and try to give them for their little play a joke — an old wheeze — about the time they caught the whale, and they cut him open — and there they found Jonah seated on that stool selling those apples three for a nickel, are you?

Slats: Wait a minute. That's not the story you — oh no, no. I'm sorry. No, I'm sorry, it couldn't be that because—that's right, he promised us it was a brand new joke. He wrote it himself, so it couldn't be that — because every little schoolboy knows that joke.

Slats: I — I'm sorry I interrupted. Go ahead. You tell the girls what they found when they cut the whale open.

Slats: Now, wait a minute, please. Give Oliver a chance. After all, he wrote this himself. If you girls can use it in the play, go right ahead. Go ahead, tell the girls — tell the girls what they found when they cut the whale open. Now, don't laugh, girls. Please. He'll blame me for this. Go ahead. No, I — I thought it was a build-up to that old joke, you know — but every little school boy knows that. He wouldn't tell that. He wouldn't dare tell that one.

Slats: Oliver! Was that the joke you wanted to tell these girls? Hmm?

Slats: Go ahead, you know the answer, don't you? Huh? What's the matter, don't you feel good? Huh? Well, you go ahead and — and tell the joke, and then we'll go inside and clean the other room. Tell it right here. Ah — Oliver — look, Oliver — hey Oliver, is something wrong? Aw, now, come on, Oliver, I didn't mean any harm.